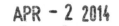

THE **HISTORY & CULTURE**
of **NATIVE AMERICANS**

The
Lakota Sioux

THE HISTORY & CULTURE of NATIVE AMERICANS

THE HISTORY & CULTURE of NATIVE AMERICANS

The Lakota Sioux

FRANK RZECZKOWSKI

Series Editor
PAUL C. ROSIER

CHELSEA HOUSE

An Infobase Learning Company

The Lakota Sioux

Copyright © 2011 by Infobase Learning

Chelsea House
An imprint of Infobase Learning
132 West 31st Street
New York, NY 10001

Library of Congress Cataloging-in-Publication Data

Rzeczkowski, Frank.
  The Lakota Sioux / Frank Rzeczkowski.
    p.   cm. — (The history and culture of Native Americans)
  Includes bibliographical references and index.
  ISBN 978-1-60413-800-9 (hardcover)
  1. Dakota Indians—Juvenile literature.   I. Title.

  E99.D1R94 2011
  978.004'975243—dc22

                                                              2010044825

Chelsea House books are available at special discounts when purchased in bulk quantities for businesses, associations, institutions, or sales promotions. Please call our Special Sales Department in New York at (212) 967-8800 or (800) 322-8755.

You can find Chelsea House on the World Wide Web at http://www.infobasepublishing.com

Text design by Lina Farinella
Cover design by Alicia Post
Composition by Newgen North America
Cover printed by Yurchak Printing, Landisville, Pa.
Book printed and bound by Yurchak Printing, Landisville, Pa.
Date printed: May 2011
Printed in the United States of America

10 9 8 7 6 5 4 3 2 1
This book is printed on acid-free paper.

All links and Web addresses were checked and verified to be correct at the time of publication. Because of the dynamic nature of the Web, some addresses and links may have changed since publication and may no longer be valid.

Contents

Foreword

by Paul C. Rosier

Native American words, phrases, and tribal names are embedded in the very geography of the United States—in the names of creeks, rivers, lakes, cities, and states, including Alabama, Connecticut, Iowa, Kansas, Illinois, Missouri, Oklahoma, and many others. Yet Native Americans remain the most misunderstood ethnic group in the United States. This is a result of limited coverage of Native American history in middle schools, high schools, and colleges; poor coverage of contemporary Native American issues in the news media; and stereotypes created by Hollywood movies, sporting events, and TV shows.

Two newspaper articles about American Indians caught my eye in recent months. Paired together, they provide us with a good introduction to the experiences of American Indians today: first, how they are stereotyped and turned into commodities; and second, how they see themselves being a part of the United States and of the wider world. (Note: I use the terms *Native Americans* and *American Indians* interchangeably; both terms are considered appropriate.)

In the first article, "Humorous Souvenirs to Some, Offensive Stereotypes to Others," written by Carol Berry in *Indian Country Today,* I read that tourist shops in Colorado were selling "souvenir" T-shirts portraying American Indians as drunks. "My Indian name is Runs with Beer," read one T-shirt offered in Denver. According to the article, the T-shirts are "the kind of stereotype-reinforcing products also seen in nearby Boulder, Estes Park, and likely other Colorado communities, whether as part of the tourism trade or as everyday merchandise." No other ethnic group in the United States is stereotyped in such a public fashion. In addition, Native people are used to sell a range of consumer goods, including the Jeep Cherokee, Red Man chewing tobacco, Land O'Lakes butter, and other items that either objectify or insult them, such as cigar store Indians. As importantly, non-Indians learn about American Indian history and culture through sports teams such as the Atlanta Braves, Cleveland Indians, Florida State Seminoles, or Washington Redskins, whose name many American Indians consider a racist insult; dictionaries define *redskin* as a "disparaging" or "offensive" term for American Indians. When fans in Atlanta do their "tomahawk chant" at Braves baseball games, they perform two inappropriate and related acts: One, they perpetuate a stereotype of American Indians as violent; and two, they tell a historical narrative that covers up the violent ways that Georgians treated the Cherokee during the Removal period of the 1830s.

The second article, written by Melissa Pinion-Whitt of the San Bernardino *Sun* addressed an important but unknown dimension of Native American societies that runs counter to the irresponsible and violent image created by products and sporting events. The article, "San Manuels Donate $1.7 M for Aid to Haiti," described a Native American community that had sent aid to Haiti after it was devastated in January 2010 by an earthquake that killed more than 200,000 people, injured hundreds of thousands more, and destroyed the Haitian capital. The San Manuel Band of Mission Indians in California donated $1.7 million to help relief efforts in Haiti; San Manuel children held fund-raisers to collect additional donations. For the San Manuel Indians it was nothing new; in 2007 they had donated $1 million to help Sudanese refugees in Darfur. San Manuel also contributed $700,000 to relief efforts following Hurricane Katrina and Hurricane Rita, and donated $1 million in 2007 for wildfire recovery in Southern California.

Such generosity is consistent with many American Indian nations' cultural practices, such as the "give-away," in which wealthy tribal members give to the needy, and the "potlatch," a winter gift-giving ceremony and feast tradition shared by tribes in the

Pacific Northwest. And it is consistent with historical accounts of American Indians' generosity. For example, in 1847 Cherokee and Choctaw, who had recently survived their forced march on a "Trail of Tears" from their homelands in the American South to present-day Oklahoma, sent aid to Irish families after reading of the potato famine, which created a similar forced migration of Irish. A Cherokee newspaper editorial, quoted in Christine Kinealy's *The Great Irish Famine: Impact, Ideology, and Rebellion*, explained that the Cherokee "will be richly repaid by the consciousness of having done a good act, by the moral effect it will produce abroad." During and after World War II, nine Pueblo communities in New Mexico offered to donate food to the hungry in Europe, after Pueblo army veterans told stories of suffering they had witnessed while serving in the United States armed forces overseas. Considering themselves a part of the wider world, Native people have reached beyond their borders, despite their own material poverty, to help create a peaceful world community.

American Indian nations have demonstrated such generosity within the United States, especially in recent years. After the terrorist attacks of September 11, 2001, the Lakota Sioux in South Dakota offered police officers and emergency medical personnel to New York City to help with relief efforts; Indian nations across the country sent millions of dollars to help the victims of the attacks. As an editorial in the *Native American Times* newspaper explained on September 12, 2001, "American Indians love this country like no other. . . . Today, we are all New Yorkers."

Indeed, Native Americans have sacrificed their lives in defending the United States from its enemies in order to maintain their right to be both American and Indian. As the volumes in this series tell us, Native Americans patriotically served as soldiers (including as "code talkers") during World War I and World War II, as well as during the Korean War, the Vietnam War, and, after 9/11, the wars in Afghanistan and Iraq. Native soldiers, men and women, do so today by the tens of thousands because they believe in America, an

America that celebrates different cultures and peoples. Sgt. Leonard Gouge, a Muscogee Creek, explained it best in an article in *Cherokee News Path* in discussing his post-9/11 army service. He said he was willing to serve his country abroad because "by supporting the American way of life, I am preserving the Indian way of life."

This new Chelsea House series has two main goals. The first is to document the rich diversity of American Indian societies and the ways their cultural practices and traditions have evolved over time. The second goal is to provide the reader with coverage of the complex relationships that have developed between non-Indians and Indians over the past several hundred years. This history helps to explain why American Indians consider themselves both American and Indian and why they see preserving this identity as a strength of the American way of life, as evidence to the rest of the world that America is a champion of cultural diversity and religious freedom. By exploring Native Americans' cultural diversity and their contributions to the making of the United States, these volumes confront the stereotypes that paint all American Indians as the same and portray them as violent; as "drunks," as those Colorado T-shirts do; or as rich casino owners, as many news accounts do.

*   *   *

Each of the 14 volumes in this series is written by a scholar who shares my conviction that young adult readers are both fascinated by Native American history and culture and have not been provided with sufficient material to properly understand the diverse nature of this complex history and culture. The authors themselves represent a varied group that includes university teachers and professional writers, men and women, and Native and non-Native. To tell these fascinating stories, this talented group of scholars has examined an incredible variety of sources, both the primary sources that historical actors have created and the secondary sources that historians and anthropologists have written to make sense of the past.

Although the 14 Indian nations (also called tribes and communities) selected for this series have different histories and cultures, they all share certain common experiences. In particular, they had to face an American empire that spread westward in the eighteenth and nineteenth centuries, causing great trauma and change for all Native people in the process. Because each volume documents American Indians' experiences dealing with powerful non-Indian institutions and ideas, I outline below the major periods and features of federal Indian policy-making in order to provide a frame of reference for complex processes of change with which American Indians had to contend. These periods—Assimilation, Indian New Deal, Termination, Red Power, and Self-determination—and specific acts of legislation that define them—in particular the General Allotment Act, the Indian Reorganization Act, and the Indian Self-determination and Education Assistance Act—will appear in all the volumes, especially in the latter chapters.

In 1851, the commissioner of the federal Bureau of Indian Affairs (BIA) outlined a three-part program for subduing American Indians militarily and assimilating them into the United States: concentration, domestication, and incorporation. In the first phase, the federal government waged war with the American Indian nations of the American West in order to "concentrate" them on reservations, away from expanding settlements of white Americans and immigrants. Some American Indian nations experienced terrible violence in resisting federal troops and state militia; others submitted peacefully and accepted life on a reservation. During this phase, roughly from the 1850s to the 1880s, the U.S. government signed hundreds of treaties with defeated American Indian nations. These treaties "reserved" to these American Indian nations specific territory as well as the use of natural resources. And they provided funding for the next phase of "domestication."

During the domestication phase, roughly the 1870s to the early 1900s, federal officials sought to remake American Indians in the mold of white Americans. Through the Civilization Program, which actually started with President Thomas Jefferson, federal officials sent religious missionaries, farm instructors, and teachers to the newly created reservations in an effort to "kill the Indian to save the man," to use a phrase of that time. The ultimate goal was to extinguish American Indian cultural traditions and turn American Indians into Christian yeoman farmers. The most important piece of legislation in this period was the General Allotment Act (or Dawes Act), which mandated that American Indian nations sell much of their territory to white farmers and use the proceeds to farm on what was left of their homelands. The program was a failure, for the most part, because white farmers got much of the best arable land in the process. Another important part of the domestication agenda was the federal boarding school program, which required all American Indian children to attend schools to further their rejection of Indian ways and the adoption of non-Indian ways. The goal of federal reformers, in sum, was to incorporate (or assimilate) American Indians into American society as individual citizens and not as groups with special traditions and religious practices.

During the 1930s some federal officials came to believe that American Indians deserved the right to practice their own religion and sustain their identity as Indians, arguing that such diversity made America stronger. During the Indian New Deal period of the 1930s, BIA commissioner John Collier devised the Indian Reorganization Act (IRA), which passed in 1934, to give American Indian nations more power, not less. Not all American Indians supported the IRA, but most did. They were eager to improve their reservations, which suffered from tremendous poverty that resulted in large measure from federal policies such as the General Allotment Act.

Some federal officials opposed the IRA, however, and pushed for the assimilation of American Indians in a movement called Termination. The two main goals of Termination advocates, during the 1950s and 1960s, were to end (terminate) the federal reservation system and American Indians' political sovereignty derived from treaties and to relocate American Indians from rural reservations to urban areas. These coercive federal assimilation policies in turn generated resistance from Native Americans, including young activists who helped to create the so-called Red Power era of the 1960s and 1970s, which coincided with the African-American civil rights movement. This resistance led to the federal government's rejection of Termination policies in 1970. And in 1975 the U.S. Congress passed the Indian Self-determination and Education Assistance Act, which made it the government's policy to support American Indians' right to determine the future of their communities. Congress then passed legislation to help American Indian nations to improve reservation life; these acts strengthened American Indians' religious freedom, political sovereignty, and economic opportunity.

All American Indians, especially those in the western United States, were affected in some way by the various federal policies described above. But it is important to highlight the fact that each American Indian community responded in different ways to these pressures for change, both the detribalization policies of assimilation and the retribalization policies of self-determination. There is no one group of "Indians." American Indians were and still are a very diverse group. Some embraced the assimilation programs of the federal government and rejected the old traditions; others refused to adopt non-Indian customs or did so selectively, on their own terms. Most American Indians, as I noted above, maintain a dual identity of American and Indian.

Today, there are more than 550 American Indian (and Alaska Natives) nations recognized by the federal government. They have a legal and political status similar to states, but they have special rights and privileges that are the result of congressional acts and the hundreds of treaties that still govern federal-Indian relations today. In July 2008, the total population of American Indians (and Alaska Natives) was 4.9 million, representing about 1.6 percent of the United States population. The state with the highest number of American Indians is California, followed by Oklahoma, home to the Cherokee (the largest American Indian nation in terms of population), and then Arizona, home to the Navajo (the second-largest American Indian nation). All told, roughly half of the American Indian population lives in urban areas; the other half lives on reservations and in other rural parts of the country. Like all their fellow American citizens, American Indians pay federal taxes, obey federal laws, and vote in federal, state, and local elections; they also participate in the democratic processes of their American Indian nations, electing judges, politicians, and other civic officials.

This series on the history and culture of Native Americans celebrates their diversity and differences as well as the ways they have strengthened the broader community of America. Ronnie Lupe, the chairman of the White Mountain Apache government in Arizona, once addressed questions from non-Indians as to "why Indians serve the United States with such distinction and honor?" Lupe, a Korean War veteran, answered those questions during the Gulf War of 1991–1992, in which Native American soldiers served to protect the independence of the Kuwaiti people. He explained in "Chairman's Corner" in *The Fort Apache Scout* that "our loyalty to the United States goes beyond our need to defend our home and reservation lands. . . . Only a few in this country really understand that the indigenous people are a national treasure. Our values have the potential of creating the social, environmental, and spiritual healing that could make this country truly great."

—Paul C. Rosier
Associate Professor of History
Villanova University

Being Lakota

Today, the people known as the Lakota live all across America: in cities, in suburbs, in rural areas, in Los Angeles, in New York City, and nearly everywhere in between. For most Lakota people, however, their homeland remains in the heartland of the United States. Wherever they may live, most Lakota trace their ancestors and their community to one (or more) of five reservations—Standing Rock, Cheyenne River, Lower Brulé, Rosebud, and Pine Ridge—all located in the present-day states of North and South Dakota. These five reservations have been home to the Hunkpapa, Sihasapa (or Blackfoot), Itazipco (or Sans Arcs), Oohenonpa (or Two Kettle), Miniconjou, Brulé, and Oglala Lakota—the seven tribes that make up the Lakota people—for more than a century. They were created in the late 1800s by the U.S. government in an attempt to impose control over the Lakota and free up much of their land for purchase and occupation by non-Indian settlers.

Before the creation of the reservations, however, the Lakota and other American Indians allied with them controlled a far larger swath of territory, stretching from below the Platte River in what is now Nebraska in the south all the way to (and beyond) the Canadian border in the north, and from the Missouri River in the east nearly to the foothills of the Rocky Mountains in the west. The landscape was harsh and unforgiving—a vast ocean of grass, sliced occasionally by wooded river valleys and punctuated by the mountainous Black Hills, where temperatures in the baking heat of summer could exceed 100 degrees (38°C) and where winters featured swirling blizzards and bitter cold that could reach 30 to 40 degrees below zero (−34° to −40°C). But it was also an incredibly rich land teeming with animal life, including the herds of bison, elk, antelope, and deer that the Lakota relied upon for food, clothing, and shelter.

For much of the nineteenth century the Lakota struggled to maintain control of this homeland, defending it against other Indians and against the mounting incursions of Euro-American soldiers, settlers, miners, and hunters. During much of this time, in fact, the Lakota were the dominant people in this region, their power far surpassing that of other American Indians or that of the United States or the various European colonizers—Spanish, French, or British—who at various times claimed ownership of part (or all) of the region.

Because of this history, the Lakota (also sometimes known as the Teton, Western, or Plains Sioux) are among the best-known Native peoples in the United States. Millions of Americans have heard of Lakota leaders like Sitting Bull and Crazy Horse, of the Lakota triumph over the U.S. Army at the Battle of the Little Big Horn (also known as Custer's Last Stand) in 1876, and of the tragedy of the 1890 massacre of Lakotas by the army at Wounded Knee. In many ways, images of horse-mounted, buffalo-hunting, tipi-dwelling, feather-headdress-wearing Lakota have come to represent all Indians—in movies, in popular culture, even as mascots

Throughout their history the Lakota have struggled to maintain control of their land. Bear Butte, in the Black Hills in South Dakota, is a sacred site for the Lakota.

for sports teams—for many Americans, and Lakota resistance to a steadily expanding United States has come to stand for Indian resistance to the political, cultural, and economic power of American society.

These popular images of the Lakota, however, also disguise a much more complicated history and people. Throughout the eighteenth and nineteenth centuries, the Lakota were both conquerors and conquered, aggressor and aggrieved. Much of the land they controlled in the mid-1800s was originally the home of other tribes who were dispossessed by westward-moving Lakota bands. Many of these other communities—including the Crow, Pawnee, Shoshone, and Mandan, Hidatsa, and Arikara—would ally themselves with the United States in an effort to stop Lakota expansion.

At the same time, the Lakota formed alliances with other Indian groups like the Arapaho and Cheyenne who shared the Lakota need for more and better hunting territories.

Similarly, Lakota relationships with Americans and the U.S. government were (and are) much more complex than is often recognized. The Lakota early on formed close connections with European and later American fur traders, trading beaver skins and then buffalo hides for manufactured goods such as guns, iron kettles, glass beads, cloth, needles, and hatchets—goods that enriched daily life and made survival in the rugged Plains environment easier. At times in the early 1800s the Lakota cooperated with the U.S. Army in campaigns against common Indian enemies. Some Lakota also profited from the movement of American emigrants across the Plains, at times supplying travelers along the Oregon Trail with guides and provisions.

As in any relationship, these bonds did not always remain stable over time. Intermarriage strengthened links between the Lakota and their Indian allies—but warfare also brought the Lakota closer to other Indian tribes, as women and children taken captive were adopted and eventually married Lakotas—with the same process happening in reverse with Lakota captives incorporated into other tribes. Lakota also intermarried with European and American fur traders, soldiers, and settlers, creating mixed-blood families and individuals who could more easily move between Indian and white worlds and serve as intermediaries, interpreters, and negotiators. Previously solid relationships could also break down, as happened when the depletion of buffalo populations strained ties between the Lakota and Americans, and as U.S. desires for control of the Great Plains led to military conflict. Even Lakota communities themselves became divided, with some Lakota working with and accepting U.S. authority and others resolutely refusing to surrender their independence.

As is the case with many Indian communities, the Lakota story is one of paradox—of people who struggled to remain free of control by outsiders yet grew increasingly reliant on goods, technologies, and organisms (like horses) that arrived via those same outsiders; who sought to live in harmony with the natural world but whose own involvement in the fur trade contributed to the depletion of the bison and other animal species that the Lakota depended on; who invited Christian missionaries into their communities yet tenaciously defended their own religious identity and customs. Similarly, though non-Lakota have tended to focus on what they regarded as the masculine nature of Lakota society and the achievements of Lakota men, Lakota women played a critical role not just in day-to-day life but also in the very origins of Lakota society.

Even the name *Lakota* can be a source of confusion. Though often used interchangeably with the term *Sioux*, the two words do not have the same meaning or origin. *Sioux* was, originally, a French version of a name used by the Ottawa, the Lakota's eastern neighbors in the late 1600s. Frequently in conflict with the people to their west, the Ojibwa called them "Little Snakes"—or "*Nadouessioux*" as the French wrote it—not exactly a compliment! Eventually, however, the term *Sioux* came into such common usage that many Lakota themselves adopted it, and it persists today in formal names such as the Oglala Sioux Tribe of the Pine Ridge Reservation and the Cheyenne River Sioux Tribe.

But the term *Sioux* also refers to a larger group of people than just the Lakota. The name also embraces the so-called Middle Sioux (Yankton and Yanktonai Sioux) and the Eastern or Santee Sioux, all of whom are culturally and linguistically related to the Lakota. All these groups are covered under the term *Oceti Sakowin*, meaning the Seven Council Fires, which the Lakota and other Sioux used to describe themselves and other communities to whom they were linguistically, culturally, and socially related. The term *Lakota* used by the Western Sioux is a phonetically distinct variation of a word meaning "allies" or "friends" and is pronounced "Nakota" by the Yankton and Yanktonai and "Dakota" by the Santee (the pronunciation of the "l," "n," and "d" sounds varying from group to group).

It would be the Lakota who would most fully adapt to the buffalo-hunting Plains lifestyle that flourished in the early to mid-1800s and whose image would come to dominate many Americans' perceptions of Indians. But the story of the Lakota people would not end with the destruction of the buffalo and the American "conquest" of the Plains in the late 1800s or with the tragic events of Wounded Knee. Instead, the armed conflicts of the mid- to late nineteenth century would be replaced by cultural conflicts, as missionaries, government officials, and other self-proclaimed "friends of the Indian" sought to prepare the Lakota for assimilation into mainstream American society. Lakota children were taken from their parents and placed in schools where the use of their native language was prohibited; traditional Lakota spiritual and healing practices were outlawed; and Lakota reservations were split up into plots of private property assigned to individual Lakota families.

Throughout the late nineteenth and early twentieth centuries, the Lakota worked to find their place in this new world. Some became farmers, others fledgling ranchers. Some converted wholeheartedly to Christianity while others (including some Christian converts) covertly kept older rituals and beliefs alive. Unfortunately, the pressures applied to the Lakota also reinforced divisions within communities, as former schoolchildren returned home after years away from their families, or as those more comfortable with Anglo-American ways began to assume greater control of reservation affairs. Even when the U.S. government introduced reforms in the 1930s that were designed to recognize, protect, and revitalize tribal cultures and communities, these reforms proved deeply divisive. Some Lakota (often termed "progressives" or "mixed-bloods" regardless of their ancestry) embraced these reforms, while those increasingly identified as "traditionals" or "full-bloods" opposed them and championed existing forms of tribal government and relations with the U.S. government (even though these were the systems that had met with such resistance in the late 1800s).

Outside events also continued to affect Lakota society. American involvement in two world wars pulled many Lakota men into the military. The participation of American Indians in World War I spurred Congress to finally grant citizenship to all Native Americans in 1924, while demands for workers in war-related industries during World War II led to the migration of many Lakota beyond reservation boundaries to rapidly growing western cities. After the wars, many Lakota returned home to their reservations, but others stayed in the cities, adapting to their new environments and a world ruled by the clock rather than the natural rhythms of nature and family life. They were joined in the 1950s and 1960s by Lakota who enrolled in government programs designed to relocate Indians from reservations to cities across the United States. This migration was part of a renewed push by the U.S. government to eradicate tribes and reservations, and terminate the unique status of tribes—based on nearly a century of treaties between tribes and the United States— as political entities outside the mainstream of American society.

In cities and off reservations in general, the Lakota struggled to adapt to a world in which Indians were a distinct minority in a larger, mostly white population. Many, facing poverty and prejudice from non-Indians, found themselves living in emerging ghettos alongside people from other tribes. In the 1960s, Lakotas joined with other Indians in the struggle to improve living conditions both on reservations and in urban Indian communities. Lakotas played key roles in activist groups like the National Indian Youth Council, Indians of All Tribes, and the American Indian Movement (AIM). In 1973 AIM returned the Lakota to the national spotlight, joining residents of the Pine Ridge Reservation in a 71-day occupation of the village of Wounded Knee—scene of the 1890 massacre—to protest corruption in the Pine Ridge tribal government and failures by the U.S. government to live up to its treaty obligations to the Lakota and other Indians.

Although the Wounded Knee occupation failed to achieve many of its goals and ended in the prosecution of several AIM leaders, the Lakota continued their efforts to obtain redress for past injustices and provide for their communities' future. In 1974 the Indian Claims Commission made a preliminary decision that the U.S. government's taking of the Black Hills—the heart of the Lakota homeland—a century earlier had been illegal and ordered the United States to pay the Lakota $17.5 million plus interest. After several appeals, the Supreme Court upheld the ruling, setting the total judgment against the United States at $106 million. Lakota leaders refused to accept the money, demanding instead the return of the Black Hills themselves. Tribal governments and Lakota educators also began to establish tribal colleges on Lakota reservations, to ensure the continued survival of the Lakota culture and language and to prepare Lakotas to participate in the non-Indian world that increasingly flooded reservations—not only economically and socially, but also through the mass media such as radio, television, and the Internet.

Today, the Lakota continue to live and assert their rights not just as Americans, but as members of separate, sovereign nations that cannot simply be dictated to, either by states or the U.S. government. Despite the disruption of older ways of life, the loss of land and other resources, and widespread poverty on many reservations, the Lakota today continue to struggle to preserve their separate sense of community, culture, and identity. In the midst of paradox, this is the thread of continuity running throughout Lakota history—the struggle to become and remain a people amid adversity and to maintain an attitude of reverence toward nature and the supernatural forces within nature in a world increasingly dominated by non-Native cultures and values.

Origins and the Lakota Universe

According to anthropologists and historians who study Native American cultures and history, the people known as the Lakota most likely have their origins in the woodlands east of the Mississippi River. Scholars base this assessment on similarities between Lakota and other Siouan languages, which include not only Lakota and its Middle and Eastern Sioux variants but also the languages of other Siouan speakers like the Catawba of the Southeast and the Ho-Chunk from Wisconsin. However, by the time Europeans arrived in the western Great Lakes region in the late 1600s, the Lakota lived in the area of present-day Minnesota and eastern South Dakota, divided into perhaps a dozen distinct villages or bands. In this region of tallgrass prairies and scattered woodlands, the Lakota traveled by foot, following the buffalo herds and either carrying their possessions or hauling them on a

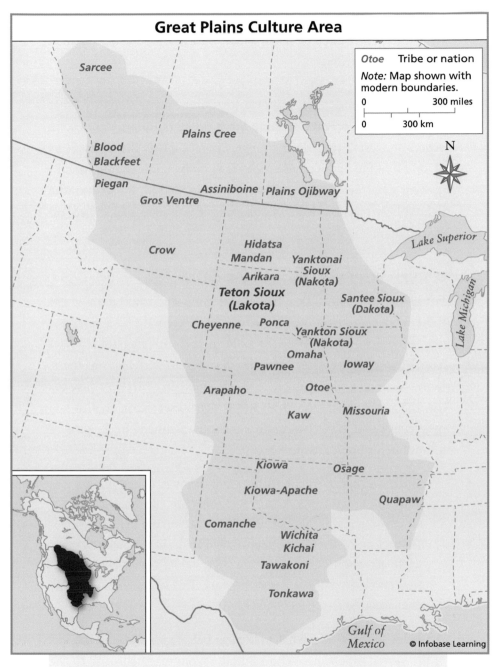

Great Plains Culture Area

Otoe Tribe or nation

Note: Map shown with modern boundaries.

0   300 miles

0   300 km

N

Sarcee

Plains Cree

Blood
Blackfeet

Piegan

Gros Ventre

Assiniboine ¦ Plains Ojibway

Lake Superior

Crow

Hidatsa
Mandan   Yanktonai
Arikara   Sioux
            (Nakota)

Lake Michigan

Teton Sioux
(Lakota)

Santee Sioux
(Dakota)

Cheyenne   Ponca

Yankton Sioux
(Nakota)

Omaha
Pawnee   Ioway

Arapaho   Otoe

Kaw   Missouria

Kiowa   Osage

Kiowa-Apache

Quapaw

Comanche

Wichita
Kichai

Tawakoni

Tonkawa

Gulf of
Mexico   © Infobase Learning

This map shows the approximate locations of the Lakota and other major tribes in the Great Plains Culture Area.

travois, a triangular frame made of wooden poles lashed together with sinew and pulled by dogs, which were at the time the Lakota's only beast of burden.

Historically, for the Lakota, the question of exact geographic origins carried much less importance. Some Lakota suggested that their ancestors originally came from what is today Minnesota; others suggested sites on the Great Plains such as the Black Hills or said that the Lakota had emerged from beneath Devils Lake in present-day North Dakota. Once, when pressed for an answer, the Lakota holy man Black Elk simply said it was so far back that "no man remembers it."

WHITE BUFFALO WOMAN'S GIFT

For Lakota like Black Elk, what was far more important than where the Lakota came from was how his people came to be a community, linked to one another by culture and kinship and distinct from other peoples. After extensive discussions with Lakota elders, James Walker, a physician who spent eighteen years working for the U.S. government on the Pine Ridge Reservation in the late nineteenth and early twentieth centuries, defined the Lakota as follows in his book *Lakota Society*:

> Those who speak certain dialects and conform to certain customs and usages are Lakota. The Lakota are allied against all others of mankind; though they may war among themselves. They are *oyate ikce* (native people), and are *ankantu* (superior), while all others of mankind are *oyate unma* (other-people), who are *ihukuya* (considered-inferior). This is the relation of the Lakotas to all others of mankind.

More to the point, what made the Lakota Lakota was the gift of the sacred pipe from White Buffalo Woman. According to the Lakota Left Heron, people once lived in disharmony with the world and with each other. "There was nothing sacred," he explained. "There was no social organization, and the people ran around the prairie like so many wild animals." When White Buffalo Woman gave the pipe to the Lakota, she gave structure to Lakota society and order and meaning to the Lakota world.

As the story was told by Left Heron and other Lakota, one day two young men out scouting for game encountered a beautiful woman on the prairie. One youth, overcome with impure thoughts, approached her—only to be enveloped in a mist that dissolved to reveal a pile of bare bones where the man had been standing. The woman—White Buffalo Woman—then told the other young man to return to his people and have them prepare for her coming.

When she arrived at the young man's village, she removed a bundle strapped to her back and took out a round stone and a pipe. She told the people that the stone—engraved with seven circles—stood for seven sacred ceremonies linked to the pipe. The pipe itself—with a round red stone bowl carved with the image of a buffalo calf, and a wooden stem decorated with twelve feathers—represented the earth and all living things, including all four-legged creatures and all the birds. According to Left Heron, the woman told the people that this pipe—the Sacred Buffalo Pipe—would bind people to one another, "to all your relatives: your grandfather and father, your grandmother and mother."

White Buffalo Woman remained in the camp for several days, but after teaching the people the first ceremony associated with the pipe, she told them that she must leave. When she left the camp, she still appeared to be an ordinary woman. After taking a few steps she sat down, and when she got up, she had turned into a red-and-brown buffalo calf. Taking a few more steps, she lay down and rolled over, getting up as a white buffalo calf. After a few more steps she turned into a black buffalo. Then, on top of a nearby hill, she bowed to the four directions and vanished.

White Buffalo Woman made the Lakota a people and a community, linked by the pipe and a shared set of beliefs about the world and the Lakota's place in it. In contrast to other religions such as Christianity and Islam that suggest there is only one origin story and one right religion for all people everywhere, the Lakota origin story was just that—a Lakota origin story. From a Lakota perspective, the story of White Buffalo Woman told how the Lakota came to be: Other peoples in other places had different stories. Even though, as Walker suggested, the Lakota could be extremely ethnocentric—critically viewing other peoples and cultures from a position that assumed Lakota ways were "normal" and natural—the Lakota did not try to force their ways and beliefs upon other peoples. Even when they did go to war to obtain land and territory, they did not force other peoples to accept Lakota beliefs.

Yet the society created by White Buffalo Woman was also extraordinarily open. One did not have to be born Lakota to be accepted as a Lakota. As long as a person was accepted by the Lakota and fulfilled his or her obligations as a member of a family in the manner set forth by White Buffalo Woman, one was a Lakota. As a result, even people who were not born Lakota could become Lakota—by marrying into or being adopted by a family and behaving in a socially acceptable manner. In contrast to nations where the government determines membership and citizenship from above, Lakota society before the reservation era was built from the "bottom up," with families as the basic building blocks.

THE POWER OF NATURE

As the story of White Buffalo Woman also suggests, both nature and the concept of the circle were critical to how the Lakota thought about the world and their place in it. What Lakota called "the sacred hoop" revealed itself in nearly every aspect of the world, from the sun and the moon to the shape of tipis and the camp circle, to the course of people's lives, with birth and death, infancy and old age linked rather than separated as in the linear timelines of Western tradition. Through the form of the circle—

without beginning and without end—all things in the world were linked to one another.

Similarly, for the Lakota the separation between the natural world and the supernatural world, which many people take for granted today, simply did not exist. Every nonhuman thing in the universe embodied some form of *wakan,* the spiritual power that the Lakota referred to collectively as *Wakan Tanka* or "great mystery"—power beyond that of human beings or mysterious qualities beyond ordinary human knowledge or comprehension. Rocks were wakan, as were the water, the sky, and the earth. Animals were wakan, as were plants. Items of unknown origin or great power that other people introduced to the Lakota might be given names linked to wakan (though in these cases the term did not convey a sense of spiritual power or association with supernatural beings). Thus, horses received the name *sunkawakan* ("sacred dog"), guns were *mazawakan* ("sacred iron"), and alcohol became *mniwakan* ("sacred water").

For Lakota, the concept of wakan governed all human endeavors. All human achievement was tied to wakan; people enjoyed success not as a result of individual skill but as a result of their ability to gain the assistance of wakan beings. Such assistance was normally obtained by creating a relationship between an individual Lakota and one or more wakan beings. Often this relationship had its origin in the performance of some ritual, as with a young man isolating and depriving himself on a vision quest (known in Lakota as *hanbleceyapi,* or "crying for a vision") in hopes that one or more wakan beings might take pity on him and grant him access to some of their power. Other ways included the puberty ritual for girls known as the Buffalo Sing; the communal performance of rituals such as the Sun Dance; or those practices associated with the sacred pipe.

Though the methods of seeking assistance varied, they all followed a similar sequence. In most cases, visions were the source of wakan power, with the beings one saw during a vision and the instructions one received from them forming the core of an individual's power. As the Oglala George Sword told Walker in *Lakota Belief and Ritual*, "No Lakota should undertake anything of great importance without first seeking a vision relative to it." Visions were different from dreams that came spontaneously to people during sleep. Normally, visions had to be sought—though they did occasionally come unbidden to spiritually gifted individuals. Before seeking a vision, Lakotas purified themselves and prayed for assistance from the spirits. This preparation often involved the ritual smoking of a pipe, because, as Sword put it, "the spirit in the pipe smoke is pleasing to *Wakan Tanka* and to all spirits." The pipe might be followed by a sweat bath (*Inipi*) in a sweat lodge—a structure made of animal hides draped over a dome of bent willow branches or other saplings. Inside the lodge, water was poured on fire-heated stones, creating steam that cleansed the body and the mind. Then, properly prepared, an individual might seek a vision.

As human beings did these things, honoring and showing respect to wakan beings through the performance of ritual and through proper behavior in daily life, wakan forces reciprocated by aiding those who called upon them. Those who had the greatest expertise in dealing with wakan beings—healing, attaining success in hunting or in war, or promoting the general welfare of the people—gained the title of *wicasa wakan* ("holy man") or *pejuta winyela* ("medicine woman").

Being a wicasa wakan or pejuta winyela was a position of great respect, but also great responsibility. Wicasa wakan instructed and conducted purifying ceremonies for young men embarking on vision quests and interpreted their visions and placed them in the larger framework of Lakota cosmology upon their return. Wicasa wakan also advised tribal leaders and conducted rituals not just for individuals seeking assistance but also for the entire community to ensure bounteous game and protection against enemies. For their part, pejuta winyela healed the sick, acted as midwives, and were also prophets. Holy people who ignored their responsibilities by failing to carry out rituals or carrying them out improperly, breaking taboos, or offending the wakan beings from whom they obtained their powers imperiled not just their own well-being but that of the entire community.

As this suggests, the Lakota did not hold themselves above the natural world. Unlike Judeo-Christian tradition, which ranked humans first in the hierarchy of creation brought into being by God, the Lakota acknowledged their dependency on the natural world—and the power that existed within it—for their survival. This belief is reflected in the Lakota story of the Great Race. According to the Lakota (and other Plains groups like the Cheyenne), it was at the Black Hills that Indians were given the right to hunt and eat buffalo and other four-legged animals. In the story told by Black Elk in *The Sixth Grandfather,* at some point in the distant past, the four-legged animals and the two-legged animals (birds) staged a race to decide who would eat whom— with humans counted on the two-legged side. As Black Elk related the story, a Lakota named Red Thunder who was present for the race was told, "If the two-leggeds win, your people will live and spread themselves and not be in want. But if the four-leggeds win, they will eat you, the people, and the birds." In the race around the hills, a clever magpie sat on the ear of the leading buffalo, and as the finish line neared, flew ahead to win the race. Afterward, the Thunder Beings who had watched the race gave Red Thunder a bow and arrow for his people to use in hunting the four-leggeds. The Lakota remembered the debt they owed to the animals who offered themselves up to humans as food, and especially to the magpie, who unlike other birds did not fly south for the winter but stayed with the people all year round.

The Lakota thus approached the world with a sense of reverence and awe. Although understanding the totality of power that suffused the world was beyond any one person's capabilities, Lakota men and women engaged in a constant quest to know more

Black Elk, Wicasa Wakan

Though the Lakota regarded spiritual assistance as essential to success in any endeavor, most young Lakota men did not acquire spiritual helpers until they embarked on a vision quest (hanbleceyapi, "crying for a vision"). However, exceptional Lakota—including many wicasa wakan—sometimes received spontaneous, unsought visions at an earlier age. As a four-year-old, the Oglala Black Elk heard voices singing that no one else could hear. One year later, Black Elk experienced his first real vision: Two men emerged from the clouds of an approaching thunderstorm singing "a sacred voice is calling you," then turned into geese and flew off. At age nine, Black Elk heard a voice saying, "It is time, now they are calling you." The next day Black Elk fell ill and, in a trance, was taken up into the clouds and granted powers from the wakan grandfathers of the six directions—north, south, east, west, above (sky), and below (earth).

Black Elk did not reveal his vision to anyone until he was seventeen, when his obsessive fear of thunderstorms suggested to his family that he had dreamed of the Thunder Beings who resided in the west. When he told his vision to a shaman named Black Road and other medicine men in his village, its power astonished them. Black Elk was a *heyoka,* a messenger and conduit for the power of the Thunder Beings. Heyokas had formidable powers to control the weather, to heal illness, and to destroy enemies in war. Under Black

about the environment, whether it be the healing powers of various plants or the movements and habits of animals. But the Lakota undertook this search for knowledge from a spiritual perspective rather than a scientific one. For example, it was impossible for the

Road's direction, Black Elk staged a public performance of the horse dance, and, after undertaking the vision quest typical for adolescent males, also performed the buffalo and elk dances to fulfill the powers of his vision. In the years that followed, Black Elk used his power and abilities as an herbalist to heal the sick.

Though too young to participate in the battles against the army in the 1860s and 1870s, the arrival of the Ghost Dance among the Lakota in 1890 challenged Black Elk's spiritual beliefs. Previously, during a tour with "Buffalo Bill" Cody's Wild West show, Black Elk had been exposed to Christianity, but the Ghost Dance, an apocalyptic-themed religion originating among the Paiute Indians of Nevada, seemed to offer an opportunity to restore the Lakota world that existed before the whites came. What came instead was the massacre at Wounded Knee. Despite his desire for revenge, Black Elk chose not to use his wakan powers to destroy the white soldiers. In the years that followed, Black Elk continued to work as a healer, even after being baptized a Catholic.

While Black Elk's story is unusual in some ways, his spiritual journey is not. Many Lakota were open to learning about other belief systems—whether from other Native communities or Euro-Americans—but sought to fit them into existing Lakota culture. Today it is possible for a Lakota to be a supporter of "traditional" rituals such as the Sun Dance, belong to the Native American Church (which blends Native American and Christian doctrine and incorporates the use of peyote, a hallucinogenic cactus, as a sacrament), and a mainstream Christian domination, all at the same time.

Lakota to overhunt or kill too many animals—people simply did not have the power to exterminate an entire species. It *was* possible to hunt in the wrong way—to fail to observe the proper rituals or pay the proper respect toward animals. If humans failed to show animals respect, the Lakota believed, animals might punish people by withdrawing from the world and not allowing themselves to be killed, with disastrous consequences for the people who relied upon them.

Thus, when the buffalo began to diminish on the Great Plains in the 1850s and 1860s—partly because of increasing American emigration across the plains but also due to Lakota participation in the fur trade—the Lakota blamed white hunters who failed to observe proper hunting rituals as well as the things the whites brought with them, including railroads and steamboats, which the Lakota claimed offended the buffalo. Meeting with U.S. treaty commissioners in 1865, Lakota representatives responded to American demands that the Lakota abandon the hunt and learn to farm by suggesting that, if the whites took away the railroads and steamboats, the buffalo would return. The Lakota diagnosis of the impact of steamboats and railroads, though baffling to their American listeners, was in some respects accurate, since both enabled white hunters to more easily ship hides from the buffalo they killed to markets, thus contributing to the destruction of the buffalo.

The spiritual basis of Lakota knowledge did not prevent them from absorbing practical knowledge about the world around them. On the Great Plains the Lakota used at least 120 different plants as food, for healing, in religious rituals, or in manufacturing items for daily use. They harvested wild-growing prairie turnips for food, pounded chokecherries into dried buffalo meat and fat to make pemmican that could be transported in animal-hide containers, steeped skunkweed leaves in water as a tea to cure stomachaches, and used spiderwort flowers as the base of a blue paint for decorating moccasins. The Lakota were also careful students of animal behavior, knowledge crucial to the survival of a hunting people on the vast expanses of the Plains. Like other Plains Indians, the Lakota sometimes set fires to burn off older grasses and encourage the growth of new grass that would attract game, and they shifted their camps throughout the year to follow the movements of the

At a very young age, Black Elk (*above*) experienced visions, which told him it was his duty to help preserve the Lakota religion. His knowledge of the Lakota religion and Lakota history was recorded in two published works: *Black Elk Speaks: The Life Story of a Holy Man of the Oglala Sioux* and *The Sixth Grandfather.*

buffalo and the seasonal availability of plants and other natural resources.

Before Europeans arrived, everything the Lakota possessed or relied upon for survival came directly from the environment.

The buffalo alone provided a wide range of items beyond the meat that was a major source of food. The Lakota used buffalo sinew for bowstrings and as thread for stitching clothing and tipi covers, and they carved bones into needles, combs, and other tools, while Lakota women rubbed buffalo brains into animal skins as part of the process to turn green hides into finished, tanned leather. Because they did not have iron pots, Lakota women cooked food in containers made from the cleaned inside lining of buffalo stomachs. Since these containers could not be placed directly over a fire, their contents were cooked by heating rocks in a nearby fire and then dropping the heated stones one by one into the containers until the meat or soup cooked or boiled.

A woman attaches a small travois to a dog in front of a tipi. The Lakota moved their camps from site to site with the seasons and with buffalo movement patterns.

Because the Lakota did not have a written language, churches to worship in, or iron kettles, Europeans were prone to define them (and other Indians) as "uncivilized" and see the world around them as an untamed wilderness. But to the Lakota, the world they knew before the arrival of Europeans was complete, and more importantly, it was home. As the Brulé Lakota Luther Standing Bear wrote in *Land of the Spotted Eagle:*

> We did not think of the great open plains, the beautiful rolling hills, and winding streams with tangled growth, as "wild." Only to the white man was nature a "wilderness" and only to him was the land "infested" with "wild" animals and "savage" people. To us it was tame. Earth was bountiful and we were surrounded with the blessings of the Great Mystery.

When Europeans did arrive, they brought with them new ways of understanding the world, and new goods and technologies that would both enrich Lakota life and pose formidable challenges to that life. As always, the Lakota would adapt, exploiting new resources such as horses to become, by the mid-1800s, the most powerful people on the Northern Plains.

The Lakota Heyday

Lakota history during the 1700s and early 1800s is a story of movement and change. During this time the Lakota went from being a pedestrian people whose only domesticated animals were dogs, and whose main importance came from being middlemen in trade between the Woodland peoples and the Plains peoples, to being the most important Native people on the Northern Plains, economically, politically, and militarily.

FROM PRAIRIE TO PLAINS, 1600–1800

In the late 1600s and early 1700s the Lakota—along with their Nakota and Dakota relatives—took part each year in trade fairs held along the Blue Earth and Des Moines rivers in what is now southwestern Minnesota. There, Indians from the woodlands to the east traded their harvests of corn, squash, and other domesticated plants for wild rice harvested from lakes and rivers in northern Minnesota and Wisconsin or for hides and dried meat brought by hunters from the prairies and plains to the west. More exotic goods—including shells from as far away as the Pacific Northwest and copper from the Upper Peninsula of Michigan—arrived with other Indians, many of them interested in trading for pipestone quarried from deposits in the Sioux homeland.

By the late 1600s, though, new items were beginning to be traded—even more exotic goods of European origin, such as cloth, glass beads, iron and brass molded into arrowheads, hatchets, knives, pots, and other tools. At first these goods came via other Indians rather than Europeans themselves as more eastern peoples obtained them from French fur traders operating out of the Great Lakes and Upper Mississippi River. Eventually, as French traders ventured farther west and began to make direct contact with the Lakota, even more valuable items—especially guns—began to be traded.

The seemingly inexhaustible European desire for furs—a scarce and valuable commodity in Europe—altered relationships among Native Americans. As hunters went farther and farther from their home communities to obtain fox, mink, muskrat, deer, buffalo, and above all, beaver furs to trade, they came into increased contact—and conflict—with hunters from other communities. Those communities that had direct contact with European traders enjoyed the greatest range of trade goods and at first maintained monopolies on guns that gave them a military advantage over communities farther west. Fortunately for the Lakota, their Dakota neighbors and relatives felt the brunt of this pressure, freeing the Lakota to expand onto the tallgrass Plains east of the Missouri River. Aided by guns obtained from the Dakota, the Lakota in the early 1700s drove the Cheyenne, Omaha, Otoe, Missouri, and Iowa farther south and west.

The movement onto the Plains produced further changes. Most importantly, it brought the Lakota in closer contact with people who owned and traded horses. While guns entered the Plains from the north and east, horses—many of them originating

With the arrival of Europeans to Lakota territory came the establishment of trading posts such as the one shown above.

with the Spanish in New Mexico—entered the Plains from the
south and west. For the Lakota the move west to the Plains brought
together the best of both worlds—guns from the east that many of
their Plains rivals lacked and horses that made living and hunting
buffalo far easier. Although the Lakota continued to trap and trade
beaver furs, their main source of subsistence increasingly shifted
to the buffalo and the associated trade in buffalo hides.

Until the late 1700s, however, the Lakota were far from being
the most powerful people on the Plains. In comparison with the
Lakota, other communities to the south and west such as the
Comanche, Kiowa, Cheyenne, Crow, and Shoshone possessed
more horses. Over time, tribes like the Omaha achieved equal-
ity with the Lakota in guns. And finally, as the Lakota (and fur

traders) pushed farther west, the old Sioux trading center declined in importance, replaced by trade conducted at the Mandan, Hidatsa, and Arikara villages along the Missouri River.

Indeed in the mid-1700s the Mandan, Hidatsa, and Arikara—agriculturalists who grew corn, beans, and squash on the Missouri River bottom lands—were much more prominent and prosperous than the Lakota. Living in semipermanent earth-lodge villages, they could travel out to hunt in the summer and winter and store much more food and produce than people who had to carry everything they owned. Village foodstuffs were prized by nomadic peoples like the Lakota because they were rich in vitamins and carbohydrates that a diet heavy in buffalo meat could not provide. For a time the lure of village life was so strong that the Oglala actually settled among the Arikara and attempted to emulate their village-based, agricultural lifestyle. Village culture even influenced those Lakota who did not begin to plant crops; Lakotas incorporated elements of Mandan and Cheyenne (at the time also horticulturalists) rituals and spiritual beliefs into the emerging Lakota Sun Dance.

But the seeming strengths of the agriculturalists—the stability provided by an economy based on growing crops and the prosperity provided by earth-lodge villages that allowed them to store surplus food and goods and made the villages a center of trade—ended up being their downfall. Along with European goods (and Europeans themselves) came European diseases like smallpox, influenza, measles, mumps, whooping cough, and diphtheria that Indians had no immunity to. Agricultural peoples like the Arikara, Mandan, Hidatsa, Pawnee, and Omaha—tied to their villages by the crops they had to plant, tend, and harvest—proved horribly vulnerable. Smallpox alone struck the Plains in 1779–80, 1780–81, and 1801–02. By 1795 the Arikara had been reduced from 32 prosperous villages to just two and from 4,000 warriors to just 500. In 1837 the most destructive smallpox epidemic of all hit the Mandan, reducing their population from an estimated 1,400 before the epidemic to just 114 survivors.

Of course the Lakota were not immune to diseases any more than other Indians. Although many Lakota did die of disease, their nomadic, horse-dependent, buffalo-hunting lifestyle made it easier to avoid the worst impact of epidemics. In fact, during the late 1700s and early 1800s—the same time that the Mandan, Arikara, and others were being decimated—the Lakota population actually grew, from an estimated 5,000 people in 1804 to nearly 25,000 by 1850.

THE LAKOTA AND THE UNITED STATES

When Meriwether Lewis and William Clark came up the Missouri River in 1804, they were well aware that the Lakota were the most powerful group they would deal with on their journey. Besides asserting American sovereignty over the new Louisiana Purchase territory, the leaders of the Lewis and Clark Expedition were eager to open peaceful trade relations with the Lakota. Unfortunately, the talks did not go well. Beyond trade with the Lakota, Lewis and Clark also sought to open trade with the village Indians, as well as with nomadic groups like the Shoshone and Crow, who were Lakota rivals for hunting territories and trade—goals that threatened Lakota dominance. After several days of tense negotiations with Brulé leaders that nearly ended in violence, the expedition moved on, with Clark denouncing the Lakota as "the vilest miscreants of the savage race."

Despite Clark's anger, the Lakota and the United States remained at peace for 50 years after 1804. In 1825, Lakota warriors cooperated with an American military expedition against the Arikara, and in the 1830s and 1840s, doctors employed by the U.S. Office of Indian Affairs inoculated thousands of Sioux against smallpox. During this time the Lakota also forged mutually profitable relationships with fur traders operating out of trading posts on the Missouri, Platte, and other rivers in the region. Some fur traders, both French and American, married Lakota women; this practice gave them a base of suppliers and customers among their numerous new Lakota relatives, while the children of these marriages, half-Lakota and half-European, often served as interpreters for and advisers to the Lakota in their dealings with whites.

At the same time, the Lakota continued their territorial expansion, pushing the Kiowa and Crow farther south and west and forming alliances with the Cheyenne and Arapaho. In contrast to American expansion, which the U.S. government led and directed, Lakota expansion proceeded without a central plan or organization. At no time during the early nineteenth century were the Lakota united politically under a single leader or government. Linked by culture, language, and kinship, each separate Lakota band (or *tiyospaye* in Lakota) was nonetheless politically independent and free to pursue its own objectives. Several factors united, however, to pull Lakota bands west.

Most important was the need for good buffalo hunting territories, followed closely by the need to replenish Lakota horse herds. By 1850 buffalo were becoming scarce east of the Missouri River due to overhunting by whites and Indians. Buffalo tended to be most numerous in the "buffer zones" that developed between the Lakota and their neighbors to the south and west, which over time pulled the Lakota in those directions. The demands of the fur trade and a growing population forced the Lakota to follow the buffalo. Lakota warriors directed most of their raids in the same direction, not only to gain control of valuable hunting territories but also to capture horses from rival tribes. Horses were essential to the life of Northern Plains Indians—especially those like the Lakota who depended primarily on the buffalo for survival.

Before the arrival of the horse, people on the Plains hunted buffalo as a unit. A community would locate a herd and stage a coordinated buffalo drive, with runners flushing the animals over a cliff to kill or disable the prey, or funneling them into a steep-sided ravine or box canyon where they could be trapped and killed. A successful drive produced abundant supplies of meat. Since buffalo could move much farther and faster than people on foot, however, Plains pedestrians also faced starvation if the buffalo moved out of their vicinity. Without horses, only limited supplies and creature comforts could be carried on people's backs or dog-hauled travois. People too old, sick, or injured to keep up with the group sometimes had to be left behind to die. The introduction of horses (originally either escaped from or captured from Europeans) changed all this. Horses could carry or haul far more weight than dogs, meaning the elderly and the infirm could ride or be pulled on a horse-drawn travois. Far more personal possessions could be carried. Thanks to the superior carrying power of horses, tipis could be three times bigger than before. And, of course, horses made it far easier for people to follow and hunt the buffalo.

By the mid-1800s, a Lakota family required at least five or six horses: several to carry the family's tipi and possessions when moving camp, a couple more for family members to ride while on the move, and one or two specialized, fast horses for warfare or running buffalo. In the rugged environment and climate of the Northern Plains, however, the Lakota found it difficult to maintain their horse herds. Harsh winters killed or crippled many Lakota horses and left even the survivors malnourished by spring. This too pushed Lakota warriors in certain directions, as they raided tribes that lived in milder climates farther south or that lived in the shelter of the mountains to the west for horses.

Typically, horse-raiding parties set out on foot in small groups, traveling quickly and quietly and attempting to avoid observation. Members of a horse-stealing party sought to avoid confrontation; if spotted by enemies while still on foot, they were unlikely to escape alive. Arriving near an enemy camp, the party would wait until nightfall before attempting to either drive off horses from the main herd grazing outside the camp or slipping into the camp to lead off the prized buffalo-runners picketed outside their owners' tipis. The raiders would then use the captured horses, switching from one animal to another as they became fatigued, to outdistance or evade pursuers.

By 1850, the northern Lakota tribes—Hunkpapa, Sihasapa, Itazipco, Oohenonpa, and Miniconjou—had pushed west of the Missouri River into what is now western North and South Dakota, southeast Montana, and northeast Wyoming, while the more southern Oglala and Brulé Lakota lived south of the Black Hills in western Nebraska and southeastern Wyoming. Up to now, Lakota migration and expansion had taken place without causing conflict with the United States. Most Americans in the early 1800s regarded the Great Plains as "The Great American Desert"—a vast, treeless, arid, inhospitable wasteland, unsuited for settlement by Euro-American farmers. That began to change in the 1840s. During that decade, reports of fertile agricultural land in Oregon began to filter east, the United States acquired California and the Southwest as a result of the Mexican-American War, and gold was discovered in California in 1848. Suddenly the West—if not the Great Plains itself initially—was valuable. For Native Americans in the West, the world would never be the same.

In the 1840s and 1850s, more than 300,000 Americans traveled west across the Great Plains. Most took the Oregon Trail along the Platte River, squarely through the southern portion of Oglala and Brulé hunting grounds. Contrary to popular images, the Lakota and most other Indians on the Plains reacted to emigrants with restraint—after all, most of them were merely crossing the Plains to get somewhere else. In many cases, Lakota and other Indians provided assistance to the emigrants—serving as guides, trading with them for needed supplies, or helping them at river crossings.

Intentionally or not, however, the emigrants brought chaos to Indian country. They reintroduced old diseases like smallpox and transmitted new ones like cholera that killed thousands of Indians. Lakota winter counts (a calendrical device that depicted the most important event of each year, usually drawn on a buffalo hide) denoted 1844 as a "small pox year," 1849 as "many died of cramps" (probably cholera), and 1850 as "the big smallpox winter." Emigrants also killed or scared off game, while their oxen, horses, and other livestock devoured the grass along the trail and the emigrants themselves consumed scarce and valuable timber with their campfires. By the early 1850s the Platte River valley—formerly a key Oglala and Brulé hunting ground—had become a barren wasteland. For the first time some Lakota began to find themselves dependent upon Americans for the basics of survival, and tensions between the Lakota and whites began to rise.

To prevent conflict from breaking out, American officials summoned delegations from the Lakota and other Plains tribes to a conference in 1851 at Horse Creek on the Platte River, just east of Fort Laramie. The goal was to end intertribal warfare and ensure the safety of emigrants heading west. More than 10,000 Indians—Lakota, Cheyenne, Crow, Shoshone, Arapaho,

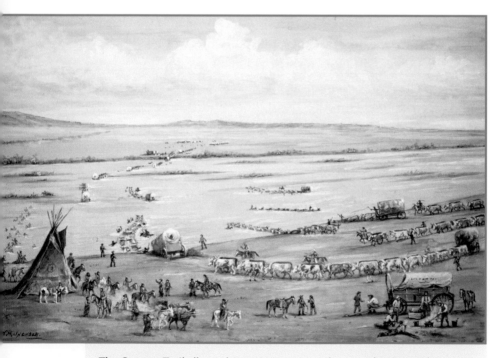

The Oregon Trail allowed Americans to travel across the Great Plains and settle in the West. At first, the Lakota had no objection to their guests, frequently showing them hospitality.

Assiniboine, Mandan, Hidatsa, and Arikara—gathered for 18 days of conferences, councils, feasts, dances, and visits. American officials worked out boundaries for each tribe and extracted promises to maintain peace among the tribes and safe passage for emigrants in return for $50,000 in treaty goods (known as annuities) for 50 years.

The final treaty recognized Lakota dominance over a vast region: all of present-day South Dakota west of the Missouri River and a portion of southwestern North Dakota; northwest Nebraska south to the North Platte River; and west to the Powder River in eastern Wyoming and Montana. Yet the treaty was deeply flawed. The six Lakota leaders who signed the treaty doubtless did so with good intent, but they had no way of forcing their followers to obey it—nor to force any Lakota leaders who had not signed to respect it. Additionally, because most of the Lakota at Horse Creek came from southern Lakota groups like the Oglala and Brulé, much of the land claimed by more northern Lakota groups like the Hunkpapa, Miniconjou, and Itazipco was not included in the Lakota territory defined by the treaty. Nor did the fixed boundaries of tribal territories allow the fluidity that hunting— particularly in the buffalo-rich border regions between tribes— demanded. Finally, longstanding Lakota rivals like the Pawnee and the Omaha were not invited or included in treaty councils. Despite all this, a number of Lakota bands managed to peacefully share disputed hunting grounds with the Crow for several years, and the Lakota generally avoided confrontations with emigrants crossing their territory.

Then in 1854, a young Miniconjou Lakota visiting relatives in a Brulé village near Fort Laramie killed a stray cow trailing behind a Mormon wagon train en route to Salt Lake City. Though Conquering Bear, the leader of the village, offered the cow's owner compensation, Army Lt. John Grattan led a detachment of 29 soldiers and a cannon out to demand the arrest of the Miniconjou offender. When negotiations broke down, Grattan's men opened fire, killing

Luke Lea Describes the Government's Plans for Plains Indians

The Fort Laramie Treaty of 1851 was designed to maintain peace between Plains tribes and Americans, but it was also intended to begin the process of transforming Plains Indians like the Lakota from hunters to farmers. As the country grew and perceptions of the West changed, American officials felt they could no longer afford to have half the country occupied by nomadic, "uncivilized" Indians. Turning Indians into farmers would free up most of the West for American settlement, since farming required far less land than the vast hunting territories most tribes claimed. In 1850, even before the grand treaty council at Horse Creek, Commissioner of Indian Affairs Luke Lea described future U.S. government plans for the "wilder tribes" of Plains Indians as follows:

It is indispensably necessary that they be placed in positions where they can be controlled, and finally compelled by stern necessity to resort to agricultural labor or starve. . . . [I]t is only under such circumstance that his haughty pride can be subdued, and his wild energies trained to the more ennobling pursuits of civilized life. There should be assigned to each tribe, for a permanent home, a country adapted to agriculture, of limited extent and well-defined boundaries; within which all, with occasional exceptions, should be compelled constantly to remain until such time as their general improvement and good conduct may supersede the necessity of such restrictions. In the mean time, the government should cause them to be supplied with stock, agricultural implements, and useful materials for clothing, encourage and assist them in the erection of comfortable dwellings, and secure to them the means and facilities of education, intellectual, moral, and religious.

Source, Commissioner of Indian Affairs Annual Report, 1850

Conquering Bear. Enraged Lakota swarmed the detachment, killing Grattan and all his men. In response to the so-called Grattan Massacre, the United States dispatched more troops to the Plains under General William Harney. On September 3, 1855, Harney attacked a Lakota village at Ash Hollow, killing 86 Lakota men, women, and children, and capturing 70 others.

Stunned by the destruction of Harney's campaign, at least 5,000 Lakota met in 1857 in an unprecedented council near Bear Butte on the edges of the Black Hills. In attendance were the future leaders of Lakota resistance: a rising Oglala war leader (*blotahunka*) named Red Cloud; the Hunkpapa wicasa wakan Sitting Bull; and a 16-year-old Oglala youth named Crazy Horse, a member of the camp attacked at Ash Hollow who had been out hunting that day and returned to find dead women and children among charred tipis. The assembled bands pledged not to allow the whites to build any more roads or forts in Lakota country and to resume warfare against the Crow for better hunting grounds. As with the 1851 Horse Creek Treaty, however, not all Lakota were in agreement. Some, like the Brulé leader Spotted Tail, were wary of American power and counseled against armed resistance. Others began to drift closer to the forts and newly established government agencies, either dependent upon American goods for survival or hoping to learn a new way of living as the buffalo became scarcer.

But American pressure on the Lakota lands only increased in the 1860s. An uprising by Dakota Sioux in Minnesota in 1862 brought more U.S. troops onto the Plains, clashing with Lakota sheltering their fleeing relations. Additionally, new gold discoveries in Colorado, Idaho, and Montana brought more emigrants. Besides those traveling west along the Platte, others followed new emigrant trails across the Plains or traveled up the Missouri River on steamboats that consumed vast quantities of wood. The new emigration sparked conflicts with the Lakota in the north and the Cheyenne in the south, leading to incidents like the Sand Creek Massacre, in which Colorado militia attacked a peaceful Cheyenne village in 1864, killing some 250 men, women, and children.

One trail in particular raised tensions. The Bozeman Trail left the Oregon Trail west of Fort Laramie and ran west and north to the Montana goldfields through the Powder River Country—the richest remaining game region on the Northern Plains.

The United States had recognized Lakota ownership of part of the Powder River Country in the Treaty of 1851, and the Lakota had recently wrested control of the rest of the area from the Crow Indians. In 1865 army troops invaded the Powder River Country, attacking Lakota, Arapaho, and Cheyenne camps in the region. In 1866, U.S. commissioners came to Fort Laramie to negotiate permission for the Bozeman Trail. Even as talks got under way, however, more U.S. troops arrived to occupy and build forts along the trail. Incensed that troops had moved in even before permission for the trail had been given, most Lakota leaders left the talks.

Soldiers constructed three forts—Forts Reno, Phil Kearny, and C.F. Smith—along the trail. For two years the Lakota, Cheyenne, and Arapaho fought to drive the troops out. In December 1866 they wiped out an 80-man detachment sent from Fort Phil Kearny under Capt. William J. Fetterman, but they also suffered defeats at the Wagon Box Fight near Fort Phil Kearny and the Hayfield Fight near Fort C.F. Smith in the summer of 1867. The Lakota and their allies, however, succeeded in stopping emigrant traffic on the trail and effectively isolated the soldiers in the forts for long stretches of time.

In 1868 U.S. commissioners returned to Fort Laramie, prepared to give up the Bozeman Trail. Talks began in the summer; but many leaders of the Indian resistance—including Red Cloud and Man Afraid of His Horses—refused to sign the proposed treaty until the hated forts were abandoned later that year. The Fort Laramie Treaty of 1868 set aside land west of the Missouri River—basically the western half of what is now South Dakota—as the "Great Sioux Reservation" and stated that none of the reservation could be sold without the permission of three-fourths of all adult Lakota men. According to the treaty, the region south of the Great Sioux

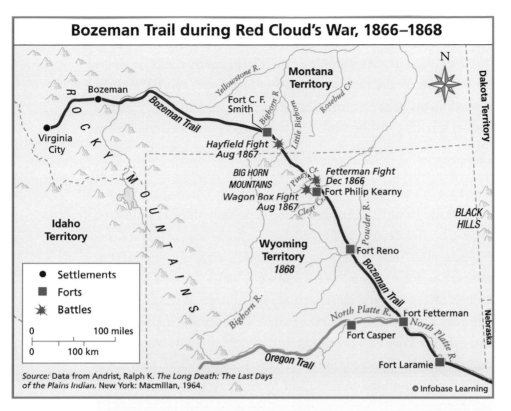

Bozeman Trail during Red Cloud's War, 1866–1868

Source: Data from Andrist, Ralph K. *The Long Death: The Last Days of the Plains Indian.* New York: Macmillan, 1964.

© Infobase Learning

Red Cloud's War began when prospectors started using the Bozeman Trail to reach Montana to mine gold. The trail passed through Lakota land, and the Indians attacked the trespassers, forcing the U.S. government to surrender the trail.

Reservation extending through western Nebraska and into northeast Colorado was set aside as hunting grounds that the Lakota and their allies could use "so long as the buffalo may range thereon in such numbers as to justify the chase." Additionally, the Powder River Country was designated as "unceded Indian territory" that the Lakota and their Cheyenne and Arapaho allies could occupy indefinitely.

On the surface the treaty appeared to be a great victory for the Lakota, actually expanding the boundaries of their territory beyond that of the Treaty of 1851. But according to the legal terms of the treaty (which it is unlikely the Lakota fully understood), only the Great Sioux Reservation officially "belonged" to them. The hunting territories south of the reservation would be theirs only as long as the rapidly decreasing buffalo remained, and the three-fourths consent provision did not extend to the "unceded Indian territory" to the west. The treaty also permitted the United States to build wagon roads and railroads through the region as it deemed necessary, as long as it paid compensation for any damages.

For the Lakota the Treaty of 1868 represented the culmination of a successful defense of the Indians' land and way of life; indeed, the Bozeman Trail conflict (or Red Cloud's War) was the greatest military victory Native Americans would ever attain against the United States. For the American representatives it was a setback, but only a temporary one to the path of extending American control over the West and preparing the Lakota for a new life once the buffalo had disappeared. Even after the Bozeman Trail was abandoned, new conflicts were certain to arise over these conflicting goals.

Life Inside the Circle

The first glimpse a Lakota child had of the world was most likely of the inside of the tipi where he or she was born. The circular form of the tipi was an appropriate place for birth to take place, being the first of many concentric circles—expanding outward from the tipi and one's parents to the larger ring of relatives and associated families who made up the band (or tiyospaye in Lakota) that an individual Lakota belonged to, to the Lakota tribe (Oglala, Hunkpapa, etc.) that a particular band was a part of, and finally to the larger Lakota community and the other peoples with whom the Lakota interacted.

After being cleansed and introduced to their father, mother, and other relatives, Lakota infants spent much of their first year bundled in a cradleboard—a wood-framed baby carrier stuffed with dried moss, grass, or powdered buffalo dung in place of a diaper. The cradleboard enabled mothers to take their infants along with them as they performed their daily routines. Mothers had primary responsibility as child rearers in a Lakota community—for girls until they married and for boys until they reached puberty.

A Lakota mother did not carry this burden alone, however, for most Lakota children had more than one "mother" and more than one "father." According to Lakota kinship practices, in addition to a child's biological parents, Lakota children also called their paternal uncles (the father's brothers) "father" and their maternal aunts (the mother's sisters) "mother" as well—a practice that gave Lakota children additional protection should one or both birth parents die. Lakota children thus grew up in a world filled with caring, nurturing relatives, as well as a world filled with far more brothers and sisters (including those of maternal aunts and paternal uncles) than most European children.

As soon as they were old enough, Lakota children enjoyed the run of the camp, since in most instances relatives were scattered throughout the community to keep an eye on them. Most boys and girls played gender-specific games that mimicked the roles they would play as adults. The choice of games and play, however, was not forced upon them. A few Lakota males chose to take on the roles of women, becoming what were known as *winktes* (men who dressed like women and assumed female roles and behavior). Winktes were not necessarily homosexual, nor were they normally stigmatized in Lakota society. Many winktes were regarded as individuals with particular wakan powers related to childbirth, child rearing, or prophecy.

Lakota children were typically not subjected to physical discipline; instead, wayward children were gently reproved and if necessary shamed by one or more of their numerous elder relatives. As they grew older, boys and girls were given increasing responsibilities in camp; boys herded the horses, developed their skills as riders, and practiced hunting small game like birds and rabbits. For their part, girls assisted their mothers in cooking, tanning hides, and making items such as moccasins, clothing, and new tipi covers.

Among the most important training Lakota children received was instruction in proper behavior. Boys and girls were taught to treat each other with respect; they were told that differences in the roles of men and women did not make one better than or inferior to the other. Children also absorbed lessons in appropriate ways of speaking to others; in conversation with relatives direct use of a person's name was avoided and kinship terms—"uncle," "mother," "grandfather"—were used instead. Behavior was also dictated by kinship. With some individuals Lakota maintained what were sometimes called "joking relationships" in which casual, even risqué language could be used, while with other relatives—the parents of one's spouse and siblings of the opposite sex, for example—proper behavior demanded strict courtesy in conversation.

In a society linked by kinship, being a good relative took priority over all else, and children early on were taught the four cardinal virtues of Lakota society: bravery, fortitude, generosity, and wisdom. Courage and endurance were essential for a people often engaged in conflict and for whom survival depended upon movement and the uncertain returns of hunting and gathering. Generosity meant placing the well-being of others and the community ahead of oneself; among the Lakota, individuals gained status not by accumulating goods but by giving goods away to the less fortunate. In his biography, the Miniconjou White Bull recalled being told by his father, "Keep an even temper and never be stingy with food. In that way your name will become great." Finally, only wisdom and knowledge—of wakan beings, in hunting, in healing, in craft work, in warfare, or in mediating disputes within the community—entitled one to a position of leadership within the community.

ADOLESCENCE TO ADULTHOOD

At adolescence, authority over boys shifted from the mother to the father; girls, however, remained under their mother's supervision until they married. Lakota girls stopped playing with their brothers or other young boys after their first period; in fact, Lakota women typically isolated themselves during menstruation, lest the life-giving power of women interfere with the necessary life-taking power of men in the hunt or in warfare. Similarly, though it was men who were entrusted with the responsibilities of leadership and maintaining order in the tiyospaye, women exerted strong authority within the household. Women owned the tipis their families lived in and all the household property; men owned only their personal clothes, tools, and ritual items. If a married couple separated, the children typically stayed with the mother, while the father returned to the tipi of his parents.

Historically, divorce was not uncommon in Lakota society. Most Lakota believed it made more sense for a couple to separate than to remain together if they proved to be unsuited for one another. But relatively few Lakota remained single for much of their adult lives. Men needed women, and women needed men. Though some Lakota married several times, the end objective for most was the same: a stable, enduring, respectful relationship with a spouse.

Similarly, polygamy (a man married to more than one woman) was accepted in the Lakota community. Because the dangers of the hunt and warfare fell more heavily on men than on women, many Lakota bands had more adult women than men. Though not a common practice, a man could take more than one wife—as long as he could adequately provide for them. In some cases a man married to one woman might take his wife's sister—usually her younger sister—as a second wife. In such families the elder wife owned the tipi and controlled household affairs.

As they grew older, the roles of boys and girls changed. Adolescent boys were invited on their first buffalo hunts and accompanied war parties as sort of apprentices, carrying spare moccasins and other supplies. In many cases, the conferring of new names accompanied these transitions from childhood to more adult roles.

This illustration shows Lakota hunting buffalo in the 1830s. Participation in the buffalo hunt was a rite of passage for Lakota boys.

The Hunkpapa boy known as Jumping Badger (also known by the nickname "Slow," for his deliberate manner) joined a war party against the Crow in 1845 at the age of 14. On the third day out the party surprised a group of Crow, killing several. Slow counted first coup on one of the Crow. Among the Lakota, as among many Plains Indian communities, counting first coup, or being the first to touch an enemy—alive or dead—ranked as a higher achievement than actually killing an opponent. Being the first to touch an enemy was a supreme illustration of the Lakota virtue of bravery. Upon his return to the camp, Slow's father honored his son's courage. Slow's father had taken the name Sitting Bull after a vision in which a buffalo bull revealed four sacred names to him. Now,

---

Plenty Kill's First Buffalo Hunt

In the mid- to late 1870s, Plenty Kill (later known as Luther Standing Bear) participated in his first buffalo hunt, which he later recounted in his autobiography, *My People the Sioux*. The day before departing with the other hunters for a nearby herd, Plenty Kill received instructions from his father. "Whatever you do, watch the buffalo closely," he said. "If you observe the buffalo to be looking at you from the corner of its eye, then look out! They are very quick and powerful. They can get their horns under your horse and toss him high in the air, and you might get killed." Plenty Kill's father also told him to ride hard through the dust kicked up by the herd until he reached clear air on the other side, and then single out a buffalo to kill. The next morning the hunters rode to the herd together so that no one would get ahead of the others and spook the buffalo prematurely. Two akicita from a warrior society regulated the hunt. All the hunters rode unencumbered by feather headdresses or extra weapons, carrying only a bow and arrows.

When the hunt began, the noise and confusion terrified Plenty Kill. "All I could hear was the roar and rattle of the hoofs of the buffalo as they thundered along. My pony shied this way and that, and I had to hold on for dear life. For a time I did not even try to pull an arrow from my quiver, as I had all I

Sitting Bull gave his name to his son and took instead the name Jumping Bull, the second of the four names revealed to him by the buffalo bull. Jumping Bull gave away several horses to other members of the band and presented the new Sitting Bull with a war shield and an eagle feather—symbolic of a first coup—to wear could do to take care of myself." Plenty Kill chased one small group of buffalo separate from the main herd. He fired one arrow into the bunch without aiming, but then noticed one buffalo cow that was not keeping up with the others. He shot one arrow into the buffalo's neck (not the heart where he had been aiming), but his second was more accurate. "Although it was not fired with sufficient strength to kill at once, I saw that she was fast weakening and running much slower. Then I pulled my third arrow and fired again. This went into the heart."

After Plenty Kill's fourth arrow, the buffalo collapsed and died. Plenty Kill was somewhat embarrassed by how many arrows he had used, remembering that his father once killed two buffalo with a single arrow, and he was momentarily tempted to remove the excess arrows from the carcass. His father, however, was pleased with Plenty Kill's bravery and honesty. Together, Plenty Kill and his father skinned and butchered the animal. When they returned to camp, Plenty Kill gave the kidney and hide from the buffalo to his grandmother, and in honor of his son's accomplishment, Plenty Kill's father gave away a horse to a needy family.

Plenty Kill's first buffalo would also be his last. Within a few years, white hide hunters armed with powerful rifles would decimate the herds, driving the buffalo to near extinction and forcing Plenty Kill and his people to rely on government-issued rations on reservations.

in his hair. (The fact that Lakotas sometimes changed their name several times could create confusion among white chroniclers— as could less-than precise translations. The Oglala Lakota Man Afraid of His Horses, for example, received his name because of his fame as a warrior; his enemies were said to be struck with fear at the mere sight of his horse. Thus, a more accurate translation would have been They Are Afraid of His Horse.)

As they matured, young men and women took on increasingly important roles in the community. Young men typically joined a warrior society, which was a type of men's club that sought to build a spirit of camaraderie among its members and competed against other warrior societies for status and fame. When a village was on the move, warrior societies were charged with guarding the women, children, and elderly against surprise attack. In camp and during communal buffalo hunts, camp leaders appointed members of one or another of the warrior societies as *akicita,* or camp police. Akicita duties typically rotated among the different warrior societies to prevent the members of any one group from abusing their powers. Young women also joined one or more of the women's groups (or sodalities) that specialized in certain crafts or served as midwives or medical specialists, or as singers for one of the warrior societies.

Such activities increased the visibility of young men and women in a Lakota community and often served as a prelude to courtship and marriage. Though their respective roles—men's mainly outside the camp and women's inside—limited opportunities for interaction, feasts and dances provided a chance for young Lakota to meet and court members of the opposite sex. Young Lakota men would sometimes wait for a particular girl on the outskirts of camp when she went to draw water from a nearby creek or river and seize the opportunity to try to engage her in conversation or play her a song on an animal-bone flute.

Generally, Lakota women—including both young single women and their elder female relatives—controlled the courtship process. Young women met suitors outside their tipis, while older women observed the process from inside. In general, young Lakota enjoyed freedom of choice in selecting a marriage partner, but parents also expected their children to choose a spouse wisely. Arranged marriages or elopements without the parents' consent were rare but not unheard of. Marriage represented more than just a link between two individuals—it also linked their families, so Lakota parents naturally preferred their children to seek a partner from a respected family, as well as a mate who possessed skills and wakan powers that held the potential for status and prosperity. When a couple married, they moved into a tipi of their own. As the head of a household, Lakota men gained a voice in the council tipi. Over time, as an individual demonstrated ability as a warrior, a hunter, a shaman, or a healer, his influence grew, and he might be ranked by his peers to serve as a *blotahunka*, or war leader. He might even be selected by a council of band elders to serve as an *itancan*, the headman or leader of the band, or a *wakiconza*, the camp administrator who appointed the akicita to oversee hunts and camp movements and maintain order in the village.

LEADERSHIP AND LAKOTA SOCIETY

European and American observers were prone to regard itancans as "chiefs" with absolute authority over their followers. In reality, an itancan's authority rested more upon his reputation for good judgment and his ability to forge consensus among the families in the tiyospaye. Unlike elected officials in American government, itancans and wakiconza had no specified term of office. As the Oglala Bad Bear told James Walker in *Lakota Society*, "If he was wise and the people found that his advice was good, then they obeyed him. . . . If a chief were brave and a warrior, then his camp would be large. If he were a coward, then his people would leave him." Although leadership roles could be partly hereditary, with a promising son sometimes chosen to succeed an elderly father as itancan, Lakota leaders ultimately remained dependent upon the will of the people.

Indeed, in many cases, an itancan's role was more to listen to and mediate than to enforce his own will. In Lakota society, decisions—regarding where and when to move camp, how to organize hunts, and whether to sign treaties, forge alliances, or wage war against enemies—were made by consensus rather than majority rule or executive power (a feature of Lakota politics that often frustrated representatives of the U.S. government, who sought swift decisions binding upon all Lakota). If a Lakota disagreed with the decisions made by the council in his band, he and his family were free to leave the tiyospaye and join another band. Similarly, political decisions made by the leaders of one tiyospaye were not binding and did not control the actions or decisions of other tiyospayes, which could make it difficult for other Indian communities or the U.S. government to forge agreements acceptable to all the tiyospayes and the families that comprised them.

At all seasons of the year Lakota tiyospayes hummed with activity: spring and fall hunts; war parties departing for raids on the Crow, Mandan, Hidatsa, Arikara, Pawnee, Shoshone, or some other tribe; children scampering about the camp, boys playing at warfare or hunting with small bows and blunt-tipped arrows, girls playing with miniature tipis and dolls made from scraps of buckskin stuffed with deer hair; women making or mending clothes, tools, or tipi covers, tanning hides, and cooking; families departing (or arriving) to visit kin in other bands or traveling to trading posts to barter buffalo robes and other hides for European or American goods, or sometimes just leaving (one suspects) to spend a quiet week or two away from the bustle of the village. At intervals ranging from a day or two to a week or more, the entire village would break camp and move to find or follow the buffalo or locate new grazing for the horses upon which the Lakota depended. Even when tiyospayes hunkered down in wooded river bottoms or sought the shelter of the Black Hills to ride out Northern Plains winters—with horses often reduced to stripping the bark off cottonwood trees to survive—Lakota tipis remained alive with life, the long winter nights enlivened with the retelling of stories about *inyan* (rock), *wi* (sun), *hanwi* (moon), *tate* (wind), and other supernatural beings.

Summer marked the peak of the Lakota ritual cycle, when the various Lakota bands and even the different Lakota tribes—

Oglala, Hunkpapa, Brulé, etc.—came together to celebrate the annual Sun Dance. The Sun Dance was the one ritual that brought the Lakota together physically, spiritually, and socially as a community. Individual men would pledge to participate in the Sun Dance in return for a spiritual favor—the healing of a sick family member or friend, or as a way to give thanks for good fortune or survival in war. But the entire community supported these individual participants in the preparations for the Sun Dance and the performance of the ritual itself.

The entire Sun Dance ceremony required twelve days to complete, divided into four-day segments. The first four days were devoted to ceremonies that for women expressed Lakota ideals of fertility and chastity, and for men symbolized roles like hunting and participation in warfare. Preparations for the dance and the instruction of pledgers by wicasa wakan occupied the second four-day period, with the final four days occupied by the erection of the central dance pole and the ritual of the dance.

The Sun Dance placed incredible physical demands on those Lakota men who participated. The most moderate form of the ritual involved dancing all day while gazing intently into the sun in hopes of obtaining a vision. The other forms all involved some sort of bodily sacrifice, ranging from having small bits of flesh cut from a dancer's arms or legs to the skewering of a dancer's chest or back muscles. In the latter case, a stick was inserted through the muscles and then tied by rawhide thongs to a buffalo skull that the dancer dragged or to the central pole, against which the dancer strained until the muscles holding the sticks in place tore free. Great honor and respect attached itself to those who had the endurance and courage to be pierced: As Little Wound, American Horse, and Lone Star told James Walker in *Lakota Belief and Ritual,* "If one has scars on his breast or his back that show that he has danced the Sun Dance, no Oglala will doubt his word."

Ideally, life within the camp—and tribal—circle was peaceful and harmonious. From childhood Lakota boys and girls were

This hide is decorated with a painting representing the Sun Dance, which the Lakota performed to show their gratitude to the sun for past favors and to request renewed protection.

taught to be unstintingly generous to the less fortunate, respectful toward elder relations, and diligent in instructing and guiding younger ones. While Lakota culture encouraged and even celebrated individual achievement, expectations of proper behavior and broad consensus kept potentially disastrous divisiveness to a minimum. Ideally, everyone—young or old, male or female, regardless of family prominence or individual status—had a place in Lakota society and had talents to contribute to the well-being of the community.

LAKOTA SOCIETY AND THE WIDER WORLD

Inevitably, reality sometimes fell short of these ideals. Rising Lakota power on the Northern Plains in the early to mid-1800s also led to intense competition among young Lakota men for status, prestige, and leadership. Young men eager to make a name for themselves in hunting, trade, or—most often—warfare could sometimes be reluctant to follow the more cautious counsel of itancans and band elders. Members of different warrior societies competed against one another inside the village, occasionally stealing wives from rivals in other societies, creating animosities that sometimes led to violence.

The fur trade also proved destabilizing. Despite the Lakota ethos of giving and generosity, the fur trade created greater disparities of wealth among families in Lakota society. The fur trade also contributed to a weakening of the position of women. The limiting factor in the trade was not the number of buffalo or other animals a Lakota man could kill, but the number of hides a Lakota woman could process and prepare by hand (a time-consuming and labor-intensive process). One result of this—combined with the rise in male mortality caused by more intensive warfare that produced a society with more adult women than men—was an increase in polygamy and a decline in women's status, as many craft items formerly produced by women were replaced with European products like cloth and metal goods obtained via the male-dominated fur trade.

Increasing contact with the U.S. government also threatened Lakota harmony. Unaccustomed to the decentralized and consensus-driven nature of Lakota politics and leadership,

American officials attempted to shape Lakota politics by appoint-
ing and recognizing "head chiefs" whose decisions would be binding on all tiyospayes. In the peace talks that followed the clash
at Ash Hollow in 1855, for example, General William Harney
arbitrarily selected Bear's Rib, a respected itancan, as head chief
for all the Hunkpapa Lakota. Harney warned Bear's Rib that he
would be held responsible for any violations of the fragile peace
between the Americans and the Hunkpapa. While this gave individuals like Bear's Rib increased status and power through control over the distribution of gifts and treaty annuities from the
U.S. government, it also placed them in the impossible position of
having to control not just the Lakota in their own tiyospaye, but
other Lakota as well, creating tension with rival leaders and young
men angered by the increasing American presence on the Plains.
In 1862, two young Itazipco (Sans Arcs) Lakota murdered Bear's
Rib for his cooperation with the Americans. Over time, with
the increasing frequency of warfare against Americans or other
Indians, blotahunka such as Red Cloud also gained increasing
influence in band and tribal councils, sometimes eclipsing more
peace-minded itancans.

Partly in response to these pressures, the Lakota in the mid-
1800s developed the position of shirtwearer. Typically consisting
of four young men from each Lakota tribe (Oglala, Hunkpapa,
etc.), shirtwearers were selected for their outstanding personifi-
cation of the four cardinal Lakota virtues. The primary duties of
a shirtwearer were to keep peace within the Lakota community
and to provide for and protect the weak and vulnerable. Yet even
shirtwearers were not immune to temptation. The famed Lakota
warrior Crazy Horse—one of four Oglala shirtwearers—resigned
his office after eloping with another man's wife.

However severe these stresses were, they did not displace
the overall principles and values that guided Lakota society. Nor
were they products of Lakota weakness. Instead, they were the

problems that resulted from the steady increase of Lakota power and prominence. In the wake of the Lakota triumph in the Bozeman Trail conflict, however, new pressures would arise that would create even more fundamental and threatening divisions in Lakota society.

A World
Transformed

Lakota victory in the Bozeman Trail conflict (also called Red Cloud's War) marked the apex of Lakota power and prestige. Not only did the Lakota force the abandonment of the hated Bozeman Trail and the forts along it, but they also retained (and even expanded) their territorial claims to the Great Sioux Reservation and the hunting territories around it. Even as the treaty acknowledged Lakota rights to their land, however, it also contained clauses stating that the United States would build schools; provide teachers, a physician, European-style clothing, and rations; survey land; and issue agricultural tools to aid the Lakota in becoming farmers, illustrating a continuing American determination to "civilize" and fundamentally transform the Lakota and the region in which they lived.

And in reality, harbingers of change were already sweeping across the Plains. By the time Lakota warriors set fire to the wooden palisades of Fort Phil Kearny, the tracks of the westward-building Union Pacific Railroad stretched halfway across Wyoming, and workers for the eastbound Central Pacific were leveling a right-of-way through northern Utah. Less than a year later, on May 10, 1869, the two railroads would meet at Promontory Summit, Utah, completing the first transcontinental railroad in the United States.

RAILROADS, BUFFALO, AND GOLD

The extension of railroads into and across the Great Plains changed the West forever. Even as they rendered old emigrant byways like the Bozeman Trail largely superfluous, they opened the middle of the continent to American industry and settlement. Within a few years, professional hide hunters like William "Buffalo Bill" Cody would be killing buffalo at a rate of more than a million per year—effectively bypassing Indian hunters and the Indian women who tanned hides by hand. In slightly more than a decade, the great herds of buffalo that provided the Lakota and other Plains Indians with their livelihood would be destroyed. In the wake of the buffalo hunters would come homesteaders and hundreds of thousands of domesticated cattle.

The changes wrought by the railroads forced difficult decisions on Lakota leaders. In 1870, Red Cloud traveled with other Lakota delegates to Washington, D.C. Sobered by the sight of massive American cities and the seemingly limitless number of *wasicus* (white men), he returned to urge accommodation to the Americans and acceptance of life on reservations. As the buffalo dwindled, many Lakota began to move closer to the government agencies on the Great Sioux Reservation, accepting government rations to avoid starvation. For some, the move to the agencies proved permanent; others came in during the winter and departed in the summer to hunt the remaining reserves of buffalo and other game. Only a small minority of Lakota—perhaps 20 percent, but including

Red Cloud visited Washington, D.C., in 1870 with other Lakota delegates to meet with President Ulysses S. Grant. From left to right are: Red Dog, Little Wound, Red Cloud, American Horse, and Red Shirt. Interpreter John Bridgeman stands behind them.

prominent leaders such as Crazy Horse and the Hunkpapa Lakota Sitting Bull—refused to come into the agencies at all.

In 1875 an even worse blow fell. Even more than the Powder River Country, the Black Hills of western South Dakota were the heart of the Lakota homeland. The hills provided shelter for the Lakota during harsh Plains winters, and their wooded slopes and valleys were sources of everything from tipi poles to game to sacred vision quest sites. Sitting Bull called the hills the Lakota's "food pack" and urged fellow Lakota leaders not to surrender them. In 1874, however, an American military expedition led by Lt. Col. George Armstrong Custer discovered gold in the hills. Though the Black Hills were well within the boundaries of the Great Sioux Reservation, the discovery sparked a full-fledged gold rush, and the U.S. government, after a few halting attempts to keep miners out, decided to buy the hills from the Lakota. When the Lakota refused, the government seized on a few violent clashes between the nonagency Lakota and whites to justify taking the hills and set a deadline of January 31, 1876, for all nonagency Lakota to report to an agency. If they failed to do so, the army would be sent to subdue them. Even had Sitting Bull and other nonagency Lakota chosen to obey the order in the middle of winter, it is unlikely they would have reached an agency before January 31.

The campaign of 1876 did not go well for the United States. Their numbers augmented by families and young men coming out from the agencies to hunt for the summer, the nonagency Lakota and their Northern Cheyenne and Arapaho allies turned back one army column at the Battle of the Rosebud on June 17. Eight days later, when the U.S. Seventh Cavalry attacked Sitting Bull's camp on the Little Big Horn River, the Indian defenders wiped out five companies under Custer entirely and pinned down survivors from other detachments for two days until other army units came to the rescue. In the fight along the river known to the Indians as the Greasy Grass, the Lakota and their allies killed 263 U.S. soldiers.

But these victories could not reverse the larger trend of events. After Custer's defeat, government officials threatened to cut off rations to agency Lakota until they agreed to sell the Black Hills. At the same time, more army troops invaded the Northern Plains, establishing military posts from which they harassed the nonagency Lakota through the fall and winter of 1876. Hampered in their ability to hunt and provide for their families, Lakota in increasing numbers came into the agencies to surrender. In April 1877, Crazy Horse led 145 lodges totaling 898 people into the Red Cloud Agency at Camp Robinson, Nebraska, to surrender. Sitting Bull held out for four more years, crossing the border into Canada to live before surrendering with 177 ragged, hungry followers at Fort Buford, Dakota Territory, on July 20,1881.

LIVING A NEW WAY

When he surrendered, Sitting Bull gave his rifle to his son, Crow Foot, to give to the army officer in charge of the proceedings. "I

A Lakota Woman Remembers the Little Big Horn

In 1876, She Walks with Her Shawl was a 23-year-old Hunkpapa woman. On June 25 of that year, she was living with her family in the Hunkpapa camp on the southern end of the Indian village along the Little Big Horn—the part of the camp first attacked by the Seventh Cavalry. Fifty-five years later she told her story to author Walter Campbell, one of several included in Jerome Greene's book *Lakota and Cheyenne: Indian Views of the Great Sioux War, 1876–1877.*

She Walks with Her Shawl was several miles from the village on the morning of June 25, digging wild turnips with several other women, when she saw a cloud of dust (from the hooves of the cavalry horses) rise behind a bluff to the east. "We girls looked toward the camp and saw a warrior ride swiftly, shouting that the soldiers were only a few miles away." Walks with Her Shawl ran back to the village. When she got to her family's tipi, her father said that the oncoming soldiers had killed her brother, One Hawk.

When the soldiers attacked the south end of the village, bullets killed several Hunkpapa among the tipis. But warriors under Hawkman drove the soldiers back. "The Indians rode among the troopers [as they retreated] and with tomahawks unhorsed several of them. The soldiers were very excited. Some of them shot into the air. The Indians chased the soldiers across the river and up over a bluff." Then news came

wish it to be remembered that I was the last man of my tribe to surrender my rifle," Sitting Bull told the officer. "This boy has given it to you, and he now wants to know how he is going to make a living." Sitting Bull's question was the same question all Lakota faced in the 1880s. Ideally, according to the U.S. government, the Lakota would have settled down to become economically self-sufficient that more soldiers had been spotted across the river heading for the north end of the village. Leaving the defeated soldiers on the hill, the Lakota and Cheyenne turned to meet the new threat. Angry over her brother's death, Walks with Her Shawl followed.

"We crossed the Greasy Grass below a beaver dam," she recalled. "One soldier was holding the reins of eight or ten horses. An Indian waved his blanket and scared all the horses. . . . On the ridge just north of us I saw blue-clad men running up a ravine, firing as they ran." Dust from running horses and smoke from gunshots made it difficult to see. "The valley was dense with powder smoke," she said. "I never heard such whooping and shouting. 'There was never a better day to die,' shouted Red Horse." The soldiers' position was hopeless. "Long Hair's troopers were trapped in an enclosure. There were Indians everywhere," Walks with Her Shawl remembered. "Not one got away."

At first, the Indians did not know who the troops were, but on the saddle blankets of captured horses, Walks with Her Shawl saw the crossed swords and number "7" of the Seventh Cavalry. After the battle the warriors returned to the camp, as did the women and children who had watched from a distance. "Over 60 Indians were killed and they were brought back to the camp for scaffold-burial," she said. "The Indians did not stage a victory dance that night. They were mourning for their own dead."

farmers—indistinguishable from the non-Indian homesteaders staking claims just beyond the reservation boundaries.

For their part, most Lakota were more than willing to meet the United States halfway. After being briefly held as a prisoner of war, Sitting Bull was eventually released to the Standing Rock Agency—his new "home." There, on the Grand River, Sitting Bull

These Sioux boys, photographed in 1880, attended the United States' first Indian boarding school. At the school and others like it, Indian children were stripped of their Indian identity in an effort to become "civilized."

settled in a cabin built by his brother-in-law, dug a root cellar, constructed storage sheds for tools and livestock, and planted oats, corn, and potatoes. Within a few years Sitting Bull had accumulated 20 horses, 45 cattle, and 80 chickens and had even been named "boss farmer" for his community by the government agent in charge of Standing Rock.

Nor did the Lakota object to the education their children would need to survive in this new world. When he surrendered in 1881, Sitting Bull expressed a desire for his son "to learn the habits of the whites and be educated as their sons are educated." After settling at Standing Rock, Sitting Bull, true to his word, sent his five children to a school established by Congregationalist missionaries near his home. Other Lakota children attended schools run by other Christian denominations, government-run schools on the reservation, or even off-reservation government boarding schools such as the one at Carlisle, Pennsylvania.

What the Lakota were *not* prepared to do was to give up being Lakota, to surrender their language, spiritual beliefs, relationships, social practices, and values. However, now that the buffalo were gone, government officials believed that Indians had to adapt to white ways or cease to exist. In his report to the president in 1889, Commissioner of Indian Affairs T.J. Morgan (the head of the U.S. government's Bureau of Indian Affairs) wrote that American civilization "may not be the best possible, but it is the best the Indians can get. They can not escape it, and must either conform to it or be crushed by it."

As a result, at schools run by the Bureau of Indian Affairs (and, eventually, at all schools, on or off the reservation, government or parochial), children were forbidden to speak Lakota. At the off-reservation boarding schools, they were also required to have their long hair cut short and wear uniforms. The Lakota boy Plenty Kill, among the first to attend Carlisle, remembered a fellow student protesting that he could learn white ways "just as well with my hair on." Plenty Kill himself, after his hair was cut and his Indian clothes taken away, was given the new name Luther Standing Bear—"Luther" from a list of names supplied by the school and "Standing Bear" as a family name after that of his father, Standing Bear. Boys at the boarding schools learned a trade, while girls learned to sew, cook, and clean like American housewives. The ultimate purpose of schools like Carlisle, though, was to separate Indian children from their parents and community for a long enough time—up to seven years—that they would forget their culture and language. As former army captain Richard Pratt, the school's founder, put it, Carlisle was designed to "kill the Indian and save the man."

Some Lakota children, like Luther Standing Bear and his fellow Brulé Chauncey Yellow Robe, thrived at Carlisle. Standing Bear returned to Rosebud Reservation to teach, and he later moved to Los Angeles, where he became an actor and author writing about the Lakota people. Yellow Robe became a teacher and basketball coach at the Rapid City Indian School, a boarding school in Rapid City, South Dakota. Despite their success in the "white" world, however, both Standing Bear and Yellow Robe took pride in being Lakota and sought to pass on their culture to their children. Other boarding school students lost their familiarity with the Lakota language and culture while at school and had difficulty being reaccepted into Lakota society. Some never returned at all: Disease and poor housing and living conditions at boarding schools led to many deaths among the students.

Much the same process took place among adults. The agents in charge of the Great Sioux Reservation passed rules requiring all adults to wear "civilized" (American-style) clothing and forbidding traditional Lakota social customs such as "giveaways" of possessions to the poor or one's relatives and rituals like the Sun Dance. Government-run courts could prosecute Lakota who failed to abide by these rules, and agents routinely denied rations, clothing, agricultural implements, or other supplies due the Lakota under treaty provisions to force individuals to comply with these regulations or to give up their children to the boarding schools. In many ways, the burden fell more heavily on men than women. While women could still fulfill their traditional roles in Lakota society, the traditional male world of hunting buffalo and serving as warriors disappeared. Many prominent former warriors joined the tribal police force, becoming, in a sense, government akicitas. Many sought to fulfill this role in a way that eased the people's adjustment to a new way of life yet also shielded them from the most intolerant aspects of government policy.

As this suggests, Lakota continued to find ways to survive. Though never completely free from dependency on government-issued rations during the 1880s, Lakota continued to supplement their diet through traditional practices such as gathering wild plants and hunting available small game and by growing gardens and raising livestock and poultry. Lakota also found employment as laborers working for the government, using their ponies and government-issued wagons to haul freight from the railroads to the agencies. Some Lakota left the reservation entirely to find work—often as "show Indians" traveling with Wild West shows touring American and European cities, including that of Buffalo Bill Cody. Show work was popular because it paid Lakota to "be Indian"—to dress in Lakota fashion, ride horses, live in tipis, and enact scenes of hunting and warfare (even if only in make-believe fashion, and with concessions to non-Indian stereotypes of how Indians were supposed to look and behave). As the most famous Lakota of them all, Sitting Bull earned the most; for one season of touring with Buffalo Bill, he earned $50 per week, plus earnings from sales of his portrait and autograph—at a time when a machinist working in a factory earned an average of $2.50 per day.

But Lakota like Sitting Bull also refused to use their earnings in accepted American fashion. Instead of building up their individual wealth and buying material goods for their own consumption, most Lakota continued to adhere to their values of generosity, sharing what they earned (or grew or bought) with relatives or the poor. Moreover, the success of some Lakota in earning a living threatened the government's ability to force them to behave in acceptable ways—how they dressed, worked, talked, and acted in general. One result of this was that the government began to restrict employment of Lakota (and other Indians) in Wild West shows. At Standing Rock, agent James McLaughlin refused to allow Sitting Bull to go on a second tour with Buffalo Bill Cody's troupe. McLaughlin also stripped Sitting Bull of his position as district boss farmer after Sitting Bull refused to renounce polygamy and abandon his second wife.

LAND, THE GHOST DANCE, AND WOUNDED KNEE

Several years of good rainfall aided efforts by the Lakota to build a sustainable life in the early to mid-1880s. A few government officials had recommended that the Lakota be trained as ranchers, pointing out that rainfall on the Northern Plains was often neither consistent nor adequate for farming. These suggestions, however, were rejected by Bureau of Indian Affairs officials in Washington, D.C., for whom raising livestock seemed too close to the Lakota's pre-reservation existence of following the buffalo for comfort. Then, in the late 1880s, the rains failed. Lakota crops withered and died in the field. At the same time, U.S. officials renewed efforts to reduce the size of the Great Sioux Reservation and reduce the already inadequate rations that now formed the only barrier between the Lakota and starvation.

In 1882 the U.S. government had attempted to convince the Lakota to sell a large portion of the Great Sioux Reservation but was unable to persuade more than a handful of Lakota to support the proposal. Under the terms of the Treaty of 1868, at least three-fourths of all adult Lakota men had to sign any land cession agreement. Then, in 1887, Congress passed the General Allotment Act (also known as the Dawes Act after its chief sponsor in Congress). Under the Dawes Act, the collective ownership of each reservation by an entire tribe would be terminated. Instead, reservation land would be divided into plots of private property—known as allotments—that would be given to individual Indian households. The goals of the Dawes Act were twofold. First, the act was intended to accelerate the destruction of Indian cultures and communities; supporters of the act hoped that giving each

Indian family their own plot of land would erode communal values by encouraging families to be more materialistic and protective of their property. Second, since most reservations contained far more land than was needed to give each family an allotment under the Dawes Act, the "surplus" land would then be sold off, flooding reservations with non-Indian settlers whose ways of life Indians, it was hoped, would emulate.

In 1888, U.S. commissioners returned, bringing with them a plan to split the Great Sioux Reservation into five separate reservations and open all remaining land—about nine million acres—to immediate settlement at 50 cents an acre. The Lakota overwhelmingly refused to sign. The next year another commission arrived with an agreement to increase the purchase price for the ceded land to $1.25 per acre and increasing the size of Lakota allotments to 320 acres. The commissioners warned that, if the Lakota failed to sign the agreement, Congress might take the land anyway without the Lakota's consent, at a much lower price. They reassured skeptical Lakota that signing the agreement would not change existing U.S. obligations to the Lakota—including the now-essential rations.

For more than two months the Lakota continued to resist, while their crops withered in the fields and hunger began to stalk their homes. When the first leaders cracked, however, a stampede of ordinary Lakota followed, afraid of being left out of the agreement's benefits. Ultimately, out of fear, persuasion, or in some cases bribery, 78 percent of the eligible adult Lakota men signed the agreement. Among the holdouts were prominent leaders such as Sitting Bull, Red Cloud, Little Wound, and Young Man Afraid of His Horses, yet even their influence was not enough. A few weeks later, the agents at the Cheyenne River, Pine Ridge, and Rosebud agencies informed the Lakota that the government had ordered a 20 percent cut in the beef ration.

Even before the land commissions arrived, the Lakota had begun to hear rumors of an Indian prophet to the west who promised to return the world to the way it had been before the arrival of the whites. After the departure of the 1889 commission and news of the ration cut, leaders at Pine Ridge, Rosebud, and Cheyenne River selected delegates to go west and investigate. The delegations traveled to the Walker River Indian Reservation in Nevada, where they met with a Paiute shaman named Wovoka (also known to local whites as Jack Wilson). In March 1890 the delegates returned, bringing with them a new religion known as the Ghost Dance.

The Ghost Dance blended Native American spiritual beliefs with Christian ideas about an end-of-time apocalypse, when the dead would rise and be reunited with the living. When the apocalypse came, the earth would be almost literally turned over—by some accounts in an earthquake, in others by a flood—the whites would disappear, and Indians and their ancestors would live in a world filled with game and untainted by disease, hunger, and death. (Whether the "good" things Europeans had brought with them, like horses, guns, and other manufactured goods, would also disappear was unclear.) It would not be necessary for Indians to go to war or commit violence against the whites to bring this world renewal about. In fact Wovoka specifically urged his followers to live at peace with the whites. All that was necessary was to perform the ritual of the Ghost Dance.

Not all Lakota accepted the new teaching. Some, including prominent leaders like Young Man Afraid of His Horses, rejected the dance entirely and urged other Lakota not to support it. Others, showing the same willingness to seek new forms of spiritual power that had led some Lakota to accept Christian baptism, looked to learn more about the dance. Some, driven in part by increasing destitution and hunger as the 1890 harvest also fell victim to drought, embraced the new ritual wholeheartedly. Though the Ghost Dance was not Lakota in its origins, it acquired Lakota elements. To the basic form of the dance (in which believers danced sideways in a large circle), Lakota added a pole in the middle of the circle, much like the central pole in the Sun Dance. Concerned about possible government retribution, Lakota believers also developed what were called "ghost shirts": spiritually endowed clothes that some believed would protect their wearers from bullets.

The Lakota's fears were well-founded. Though they were not the only Plains Indians to adopt Wovoka's teachings, the government responded to the Lakota Ghost Dance with a greater degree of force than anywhere else on the Plains. At Pine Ridge a nervous new agent (nicknamed "Young-Man-Afraid-of-the-Indians" by the Lakota) requested army troops. The agent at Standing Rock took advantage of the Ghost Dance as an excuse to arrest the Hunkpapa wicasa wakan Sitting Bull, who had emerged as a leader of the movement there. When Indian police arrived at Sitting Bull's home on December 15, 1890, a fight broke out between the police and Sitting Bull's supporters in which Sitting Bull, his 14-year-old son Crow Foot, five of Sitting Bull's followers, and six policemen were killed.

By the time of Sitting Bull's death, nearly 7,000 U.S. Army troops had converged on the Lakota reservations. The appearance of so many troops reignited Lakota fears of violence. After the killing of Sitting Bull, refugees from Standing Rock fled south to the Cheyenne River Reservation, some finding shelter with a group of Ghost Dance supporters led by the Miniconjou Big Foot. When troops arrived to escort Big Foot's band back to the agency, they too fled south, heading for Pine Ridge. Once there, Big Foot sent messengers to the agency to announce that he and his people would come in and surrender peacefully. However, army commanders, fearful that Big Foot and his people would again flee, sent troops from the Seventh Cavalry (Custer's old outfit) to disarm the Lakota and escort them to the agency. The troops met Big Foot—who by this time was suffering from pneumonia—on December 28 near Wounded Knee Creek.

Bodies of 146 Lakotas are piled into a mass grave after the tragedy at Wounded Knee. Soldiers and civilians look on.

The following day, after soldiers surrounded the Lakota on three sides, with cannon placed on a hill overlooking the camp, officers ordered the Lakota to surrender their guns. When only a few were turned over, a detachment of soldiers was ordered to search the Lakota camp. What happened next remains disputed. As the soldiers searched the camp, ransacking Lakota tipis and frisking women for concealed weapons, a wicasa wakan began to speak to the people and throw dust in the air. Accounts differ on whether he was urging Big Foot's people to resist or urging them to remain calm during the search. As the soldiers began to search the Lakota men, a shot went off.

Instantly there was chaos. Soldiers on all three sides of the Lakota began to fire; some bullets that did not hit the Lakota struck soldiers stationed on the opposite side of the camp. Big Foot, lying on a blanket, was killed almost immediately. Most Lakota attempted to flee up a dry ravine that ran west from the camp site. Those Lakota men who still had weapons tried to protect the flight of the women and children. Officers of the Seventh later claimed that they attempted to prevent the killing of women, children, and the elderly. But by the time the shooting ended, nearly 300 Lakota out of the 400 in Big Foot's band had been killed—most of them women and children. Many were killed at a distance—in some cases more than a mile—from where the shooting had broken out as they were trying to flee.

Government and military officials later commissioned an investigation into what happened at Wounded Knee, but they also approved the issuing of 20 Medals of Honor to soldiers for their actions there. At the site of the massacre, 146 Lakota were buried in a mass grave on a hill overlooking Wounded Knee Creek.

Finding
a New Way

M any histories of the Lakota end with the Wounded Knee Massacre, as if nothing that happened after that mattered. But for most Lakota, life went on after 1890. Family, community, and survival continued to be the main concerns of daily life. Despite the government's crackdown on open expressions of Lakota spirituality and culture, being a good relative—a good Lakota—retained its importance.

LIFE AFTER WOUNDED KNEE
Though children were taught English in school, Lakota remained the primary language in most Lakota homes. Many Lakota—particularly those from more "traditionalist" homes—gained at best limited fluency in the white man's language. As allotments began to be issued, the Lakota also attempted to keep their local communities intact; members of a particular tiyospaye tended

to take allotments and settle in close proximity to one another. Many wicasa wakan quietly continued to work as healers and tried to pass along their knowledge to younger Lakota. Though they remained at the mercy of the unpredictable Plains climate, the Lakota also continued to cultivate small gardens, raise livestock, gather wild plants, hunt small game, and pursue other sources of subsistence, such as working for the government or for local non-Indian farmers and ranchers. By the early 1900s, most Lakota no longer depended upon government rations for survival. As Frank Fools Crow, a Pine Ridge wicasa wakan born about the time of the Wounded Knee Massacre, would remember in his biography, "In some ways, conditions were even better than the old buffalo-hunting days. In the fall of each year we helped one another to gather the harvest and to store it in root cellars. Winters in our country had always been difficult to live through, and being able to store food like this was a proud and comforting achievement."

In a rapidly modernizing, industrializing, and urbanizing world, Indians in general ceased to be a focus of government policy. Though the rules against open expressions of Indian culture remained in effect, many government officials had long since given up on the quest to merge Indians into mainstream American society. Lakota men still needed to cut their hair short to get an agency job, but Sun Dances once again began to be held in quiet, secluded locations back in the hills at Pine Ridge, Cheyenne River, and elsewhere. When Madonna Swan's oldest brother, Manuel, was born in 1919, their mother celebrated his first birthday with a traditional Lakota giveaway. "She gave away a tipi, beaded cradleboards, saddlebags, horses, Pendleton blankets, and many quilts," Madonna told her biographer. "She gave away everything she had been given to start her married life." Officially, giveaways were still illegal, but the attention of most Americans was now on the problems of booming cities, clashes

Lakota at the Pine Ridge Reservation. Although Indians in the early 1900s were encouraged to adapt to mainstream U.S. society, they persisted in keeping their culture alive.

between workers and employers, and foreign affairs. Indians might be left to themselves in poverty and isolation on their reservations.

Several factors, however, combined to prevent the Lakota from attaining more prosperity, beyond the traditional Lakota ethos of generosity and sharing. The way allotment worked almost guaranteed that most Lakota would not only remain poor but would become poorer over time. According to the Dawes Act, when an Indian received an allotment, the title (or deed) to that property would remain in the control (or "in trust") of the U.S. government for 25 years. During that time the land would not be subject to taxes and could not be sold. At the end of the 25-year trust period, the allotee would receive the deed to his or her allotment and gain U.S. citizenship (up to now, most Lakota—and most Indians— were not regarded as U.S. citizens).

The purpose of this provision was to protect inexperienced Indians from being cheated or swindled out of their allotments by dishonest whites. Though it was intended to protect Indians, however, the trust provision also put them at a serious disadvantage. Because the U.S. government held the deed to allotments, Lakota (and other allotted Indians) could not use the land as collateral to get loans from banks to buy farm equipment or purchase livestock. Without access to cash it was difficult for inexperienced Lakota agriculturalists to compete with better-funded non-Indian farmers.

Even worse, the allotments themselves were too small. The government officials who wrote legislation like the Dawes Act were mostly from the eastern part of the country—places that received more rain and had more fertile soil than the Northern Plains. In places like the East and Midwest, 320 acres was more than enough for a prosperous family farm. Where the Lakota lived, it was not nearly enough (ultimately, even most non-Indian homesteaders on the Great Plains would go bankrupt, doomed by the same problems of inadequate land and drought). In the long term, farming and ranching on the Plains would be dominated by those individuals with enough money to work the land on a large scale—in some cases thousands of acres—rather than by homesteaders or allotted Indians.

Finally, when allotees died—most of them without wills—their land was divided up among all their heirs. A single allotment might be divided into four, six, or eight or more parcels. After a generation or two passed, many allotments were chopped up into such little pieces (and members of the second or third generation might own so many small, separate pieces of different allotments) that it was impossible to work the land in a productive fashion. What this meant for the Lakota was that in the short term it made more sense to lease allotments to non-Indian farmers or ranchers and split the rent money among the heirs, or, alternatively, to sell the allotment entirely, which began to happen with increasing frequency in the early 1900s, especially after Congress shortened the trust period during which allotments could not be sold. As early as 1922 one government official estimated that 95 percent of the Lakota who had received deeds to their allotments had lost their land.

Government policies also hampered the development of Lakota ranching. Over time, the failure of Indians and non-Indians to succeed in commercial farming west of the Missouri River convinced many government officials that ranching was the only economic strategy with hopes of success. Because individual allotments were too small for large-scale ranching, some began to support efforts to create tribal cattle herds grazing on unallotted reservation land. By 1901, the number of cattle at Pine Ridge owned either by individual Indians or the tribe itself had reached 19,000; a year later, the number had increased to 31,000. Cattle ranching became a source of pride for Lakota ranchers and cowboys, harking back as it did to the old days of hunting buffalo on horseback. Here too, however, the government began to open up Indian lands to non-Indian ranchers, and when the United States became involved in World War I, government officials pressured Lakota ranchers to sell their cattle to support the war effort. Many Lakota ranchers, unfortunately, were never able to rebuild their herds afterward.

World War I (and World War II) also brought other changes to Lakota life. Lakota and other Indians had previously served with the army, but usually as guides, scouts, or auxiliaries rather than with the regular military establishment. Even though many young Lakota men were still not citizens, they were declared eligible for the military draft put into effect in 1917. Some Lakota were drafted; others—citizens or not—volunteered for service. Service during wartime enabled Lakota not only to prove their loyalty to the United States, but also to reclaim elements of their culture that had begun to fade with the end of intertribal warfare and government restriction. Susan Krouse, author of *North American Indians in the Great War,* has noted that many Lakota would have echoed the comment of Private Joe High Elk, a 24-year-old Cheyenne River resident, who told an interviewer, "I was doing my duty as a patriot and was fighting to save democracy, and do hope that in the future we Indians may enjoy freedom which we Indians are always denied." When Guy Dull Knife left Pine Ridge for the Western Front, he wore a small sacred medicine bundle around his neck, and after Germany's surrender in 1918, Standing Rock Lakota held a victory dance—the first since the Battle of the Little Big Horn in 1876, while returning veterans provided new members for warrior societies (to this day, the grand entry at powwows on Lakota and other Indian reservations begins with an honor song for and a parade led by Native American veterans). After World War I, Congress recognized Indian service by passing the Indian Citizenship Act in 1924—finally making all Indians U.S. citizens.

Lakota and other Native Americans also bought war bonds to support the war effort, and particularly during World War II, thousands of Lakota migrated to war production centers in Rapid City, Denver, and even the West Coast, taking advantage of new job opportunities at wages undreamed of on reservations. At the end of the war, some Lakota returned to their reservations, but others stayed in their new homes, helping form the nucleus of new, multitribal, urban Indian communities. Among the Lakota who traveled to the West Coast during World War II was the family of a three-year-old Pine Ridge boy named Russell Means, whose father found work in a naval shipyard near Oakland.

LAKOTA, THE NEW DEAL, AND THREATS TO SOVEREIGNTY

Even for those Lakota who stayed behind on the reservation, the 1930s and 1940s were decades of turmoil and change. In 1928 a government report documented substandard living conditions and widespread poverty on many reservations. With the onset of the Great Depression in 1929 and the election of Franklin Delano

Roosevelt as president in 1932, reformers seeking to eradicate poverty and want from American society began to exert more control over government policy.

Among those reformers coming to Washington, D.C., in the early 1930s was the new commissioner of Indian affairs, John Collier. Before World War I, Collier had served as a social worker in New York City's immigrant neighborhoods. Disillusioned by the destruction and loss of life in World War I, Collier sought refuge in "traditional" communities he viewed as being less tainted by modern industrial life. In the 1920s, Collier was heavily involved in Indian affairs, becoming a fierce critic of government policies toward Indians and working to protect Pueblo Indian lands and ways of life in the Southwest. After becoming commissioner, Collier halted the old policy of allotment and ordered government officials on reservations to respect Indians' rights to freedom of religion and culture. In 1934, Collier proposed legislation to restore self-government to Native communities throughout the United States. The Indian Reorganization Act (IRA) permitted tribes to write tribal constitutions to establish their own governments on reservations, which would have the power to operate tribal court systems, levy taxes, negotiate contracts, and otherwise manage tribal affairs.

The IRA promised to greatly expand the power of tribes and tribal governments. But among many Indians—and especially on Lakota reservations—it also met strong resistance. At Rosebud and Pine Ridge in particular, it exposed divisions within tribes themselves. During the early reservation period, politics on most Lakota reservations took the form of what were often called general councils—large, community-wide meetings, often dominated by elders who sought to achieve broad consensus within the community. Many government agents disliked this system, believing it gave too much power to older, more traditionally inclined leaders. By the early 1900s, agents at most Lakota reservations had replaced the general councils with so-called business committees

John Collier (*center*) greets Wounded Knee massacre survivors Dewey Beard (*left*) and James Pipe-on-Head (*right*). As commissioner of Indian affairs, Collier worked to protect Indian culture.

more often comprising younger, school-educated Lakota, many of them of mixed Indian-European heritage and more comfortable with Anglo-American ways. Members of tribal business committees were not selected by consensus within their communities, but by a simple majority vote in formal elections. The power of these business committees was limited, however, since agents rather than the councils made most key decisions. In many cases, Lakota who disagreed with the decisions or positions of council members could simply go over (or around) the business council and appeal to the agent personally. The IRA (in theory) promised to give much more power to these tribal business committees.

Collier had promised that each tribe would be allowed to vote on whether to accept the IRA; referendums on Lakota reservations were set for the fall of 1934. As the referendum date approached, intense disputes emerged between "New Dealers" who supported the IRA and "Old Dealers" who rejected it and often sought a return to the old system of general councils. Eventually, every Lakota reservation voted in favor of the IRA. Many Lakota, however, did not even participate in the election. At Pine Ridge just 55 percent of eligible voters cast ballots; at Rosebud, just 40 percent. Even though the IRA passed on both reservations, it was approved by just 29 and 27 percent, respectively, of the voting age population. Why did so few Lakota vote?

Possible explanations lie in the old 1868 Fort Laramie Treaty and the consensus-driven nature of traditional Lakota politics. Under the Treaty of 1868 major decisions such as land cessions had to be approved by three-quarters of all adult Lakota men; additionally, in traditional Lakota politics refusal to participate in making a decision represented a way of saying "no" to whatever was being proposed. If a consensus could not be reached, no action would be taken. Many Lakota who either disapproved of the IRA or didn't think they knew enough to make a decision may have simply refused to vote. However, in the Anglo-American political model the referendums were based on, all that was required was a simple majority of those who *did* vote—and as a result, supporters of the IRA carried the day.

Unfortunately, the new IRA tribal councils were not as independent of the Bureau of Indian Affairs as had been promised. Every decision the tribal councils made had to be approved by the commissioner of Indian affairs. Within the tribe, however, the new councils exerted more power over tribal members than ever before. Although many tribal councilmen sought to serve the whole community, others looked out mainly for themselves, their relatives, and their political supporters. Few were in a position to strongly contest policies proposed by the federal government. As

Robert Burnette (himself a former chairman of the Rosebud IRA tribal council) put it in his book *The Road to Wounded Knee,* the internally powerful but externally powerless new governments were "a blueprint for elected tyranny."

Even Collier's respect for Indian communities and culture would not survive the 1930s. With the coming of World War II and the Cold War with the Soviet Union that followed, the emphasis of government policy once again shifted toward one of conformity to "mainstream" American values. In 1942 the U.S. government leased 122,000 acres of land on Pine Ridge for use as a bombing and gunnery range for training by the Army Air Force. More than 100 families had to be relocated, with the land remaining dangerous long afterward due to the presence of unexploded bombs and other ammunition. After the war, the U.S. Army Corps of Engineers and federal Bureau of Reclamation began a series of dam-building projects along the Missouri River. To avoid flooding largely non-Indian cities like Bismarck, North Dakota, and Pierre, South Dakota, the dams were built directly downstream from Indian reservations. The Oahe Dam alone flooded more than 160,000 acres of land on the Standing Rock and Cheyenne River reservations. The most valuable land on the reservations—containing the most fertile soil, 90 percent of the timber supply, and a main source of game and wild plants the Lakota still harvested and depended upon—was swallowed up by the rising waters. More than 20 percent of the reservations' population had to be relocated. The government did pay the Lakota for the land but at rates it determined, with little regard to the land's actual value to the Lakota.

Finally, in the 1950s the government targeted tribes themselves, designing policies dubbed "termination" and "relocation" to end the special legal status of tribes, reservations, and Indians, and to merge Native Americans into an increasingly urban American society. Termination threatened even the limited self-rule offered by the IRA by proposing to make tribes and reservation land subject to state jurisdiction, while relocation sought

Life on and off the Reservation

Celene Not Help Him (born in 1928) and Cecilia Hernandez Montgomery (born in 1910) were both born and raised on the Pine Ridge Indian Reservation. In 1945, Montgomery and her husband moved to Rapid City, South Dakota. In Sarah Penman's *Honor the Grandmothers: Dakota and Lakota Women Tell Their Stories,* the two Oglala women offer a look at what life was like for Lakota on and off the reservation in the mid-1900s.

Celene Not Help Him was raised by her grandparents after her father died when she was fourteen months old. Her grandparents ran a horse ranch with more than 1,000 head of horses, but they were forced to move in 1942 when the U.S. government took their land for an aerial bombing and gunnery range. "We have to move out of there within 30 days," Not Help Him recalled. "We had [retrieved] only four head of horses out of that thousand head; we lost everything. So that's why I say Grandpa got massacred two times by army; first, at that Wounded Knee, and the second time [when] we have to move out of that place for the Air Force." After the war the land was turned over to the Oglala Sioux Tribe rather than to its former owners. "I check over there and they want more than $400 [for the land]; we have to have that much to deposit but I haven't got that kind of money. So it belongs to the tribe now and I don't have a home."

Cecilia Hernandez Montgomery also grew up in a rural portion of Pine Ridge; her family ranched cattle and

to accelerate Indian migration from reservations to urban centers by offering incentives that included job placement, housing assistance, and one year of medical care.

Even though many Lakota had already moved off the reservation either temporarily or permanently, the relocation program gardened. Like most Lakota, her parents' home had neither electricity nor indoor plumbing. "We used kerosene lamps and we used a wood stove. There was a lot of laundry to be done and we used to wash this all by hand with those great big old-time washboards. . . . Oh, I dreaded wash days." Hernandez Montgomery attended Genoa Indian School in Genoa, Nebraska, and married a Crow Indian she met there. After her mother died, she and her husband moved off the reservation—first to Nebraska and then to Rapid City. "We found jobs in Nebraska. The town of Gordon was small at that time but they were really what you'd call racist. We were going to go in and eat in a little café, and here it had a big sign on there said 'No Indians Allowed.'" Attitudes weren't much better in Rapid City; when Hernandez Montgomery applied for a job as a dishwasher in a hotel, she was told, "'Sorry, we don't hire Indians.' . . . That was my first taste then, my first experience."

Both Not Help Him and Hernandez Montgomery became active in their Indian communities. Not Help Him became a disc jockey at KILI radio—an Indian-owned and -operated radio station on Pine Ridge, while Hernandez Montgomery helped found programs to provide meals for low-income elderly and improve housing conditions for Indians living in Rapid City. "We finally woke up to the fact that we have to stand up for ourselves," Hernandez Montgomery said, "[be]cause nobody else is going to do it; we have to be heard."

attempted to sever ties between Indians and their home communities by moving them as far away as possible. Rather than move Lakota to Rapid City, Denver, or Minneapolis, for example, relocation often sent Lakota to Chicago, Phoenix, or Los Angeles. As with boarding schools a half-century before, some Lakota thrived in these new environments, while others struggled to adapt to a world ruled by clock time and the demands of employers rather than that of family and kin. Successful or not, most faced prejudice and racism in largely non-Indian communities.

Closer to home, although no Lakota tribes were directly targeted for termination by the federal government, the Lakota and other Indian tribes did have to fend off several attempts by the state of South Dakota to assume criminal and civil jurisdiction over Indian communities and land in the 1950s and 1960s. Even on the reservations, government officials and Christian ministers— some of them Lakota themselves—continued to apply pressure for assimilation. "I had one teacher in fourth or fifth grade who flat out told us that we were a conquered nation, a conquered people," Guy Dull Knife Jr. recalled in *The Dull Knifes of Pine Ridge*. "If we didn't give up our language and stop the devil worship [i.e., traditional Lakota religion], he said, none of us would ever amount to anything. Most of the BIA teachers were like him." Even though the wars of the 1800s were over, the Lakota still struggled to survive as a people and as a community.

Return to Wounded Knee

I n the darkness of the evening of February 27, 1973, a small caravan of cars and vans drove over the country roads of the Pine Ridge Indian Reservation. In the vehicles were members and supporters of the American Indian Movement (AIM)—some Lakota, some not. Originally formed in 1968 by Indians in Minneapolis, Minnesota, to monitor police treatment of Native Americans in that city, AIM had become a national movement notorious for its militant language and spectacular protests, including participation in a 1970 Thanksgiving protest at Plymouth Rock in Massachusetts and a 1972 takeover of the headquarters of the Bureau of Indian Affairs in Washington, D.C.

AIM first came to Pine Ridge in the spring of 1972, following the death of Raymond Yellow Thunder. Yellow Thunder died in February 1972 in Gordon, Nebraska, a border town littered with bars and liquor stores just off the Pine Ridge Reservation (where alcohol sales were prohibited). A gentle 51-year-old cowboy from the Porcupine community on Pine Ridge, Yellow Thunder had been attacked by four white men, beaten, stripped of his clothes, thrown in the trunk of a car, and forced into a crowded American Legion hall. After the attack, Yellow Thunder managed to make it back to his pickup truck, where he died of exposure and head injuries. Angered by the local district attorney's handling of the case (calling it a "cruel practical joke" carried out by "pranksters"), members of the Porcupine community contacted Russell Means, whose family originally came from Porcupine, to bring AIM to Gordon. For three days, AIM members and Pine Ridge residents carried out vigorous protests in Gordon. The following winter, AIM led protests in Rapid City and Custer, South Dakota, in the Black Hills following the fatal stabbing of another Pine Ridge resident, Wesley Bad Heart Bull, by a white man.

Although most of AIM's founders were non-Lakota from cities, not reservations (even Means, though born on Pine Ridge, did not speak Lakota), AIM's involvement in civil rights protests on and near Pine Ridge—and the founding of AIM chapters at Pine Ridge—inevitably involved the organization in the growing political dispute between supporters and opponents of the Pine Ridge tribal government led by Richard "Dick" Wilson. In certain ways, the origins of the dispute went all the way back to the passage of the Indian Reorganization Act and the tension between those who advocated a "traditional" form of government and relationship between Lakota communities and the United States and those who supported elected, majority-rule tribal councils. The dispute intensified in the late 1960s, when increased federal funding for social programs aimed at reducing poverty and increasing economic development began to arrive at Pine Ridge, with the tribal council and tribal chairman controlling the funds and determining who got jobs or otherwise benefited from the programs. Wilson's opponents accused him of corruption and nepotism in steering jobs and benefits to his supporters.

As tribal chairman, Wilson also enjoyed the official support of the U.S. government. As tensions between Wilson and AIM (and a newly created organization known as the Oglala Sioux Civil Rights Organization, or OSCRO) grew, federal marshals and FBI agents were dispatched to Pine Ridge. Wilson also used federal funds to create an auxiliary tribal police force (dubbed the "goons" by many Oglala) that allegedly beat up and intimidated his opponents. When an attempt to impeach Wilson and remove him from office on February 22 failed, OSCRO and AIM supporters met in a village hall in the small, traditionalist community of Calico, to plan their next move.

In her autobiography, Mary Crow Dog, a Brulé AIM supporter from Rosebud, wrote, "It was the older women like Ellen Moves Camp and Gladys Bissonette who first pronounced the magic words, 'Wounded Knee.'" The occupation of the site—by then the location of a white-owned trading post that sold trinkets, including postcards with images of frozen Lakota bodies from the 1890 massacre—was also endorsed by several elder Oglala traditional chiefs and holy men. "Take your brothers from the American Indian Movement and go to Wounded Knee and make your stand there," said Frank Fools Crow, a noted wicasa wakan. When the protesters arrived at Wounded Knee—seizing the trading post and building fortifications to defend themselves from Wilson's goons and federal agents—Crow Dog remembered one Oglala shouting in triumph, "We hold the Knee!"

The resulting standoff at Wounded Knee between AIM, OSCRO, and the Wilson administration and U.S. government lasted 71 days. During the siege the occupiers proclaimed the formation of the Independent Oglala Nation and called for a return to nineteenth-century treaty relations between Lakota communities and the United States. Periodic firefights broke out between the occupiers (who possessed a small number of mostly ineffective weapons) and the heavily armed federal marshals; during the shoot-outs two protesters were killed. Indians and non-Indians

AIM leader Russell Means (*left*) and assistant U.S. attorney general Kent Frizzell (*right*) sign the settlement of the Wounded Knee occupation on April 5, 1973.

sympathetic to the occupiers' cause attempted to smuggle in food and other essential supplies through the cordon set up by federal officials and Wilson's police. Finally on May 8 the protesters agreed to surrender. Many of the occupiers had already departed, scattering into the Pine Ridge countryside; those who remained faced arrest and prosecution.

AFTER (AND BEFORE) WOUNDED KNEE

The siege at Wounded Knee riveted the nation's attention upon Pine Ridge and the problems of Indians in America in general. But the standoff itself did not really resolve anything. Political unrest continued at Pine Ridge; in 1974 Dick Wilson became the first Oglala Sioux tribal chairman ever to win reelection, in a campaign marked by violence, accusations of voter fraud, and more than a dozen unresolved deaths. In 1975, a shoot-out between AIM members and officers from the Federal Bureau of Investigation led to the deaths of two FBI agents. In a controversial trial Leonard Peltier, a Dakota-Chippewa AIM member, was convicted of murder and sentenced to life in prison. The U.S. government cracked down on AIM and its supporters, eventually arresting 562 people for events in connection with the siege. The trials lasted two years. Judges threw out some of the charges due to government misconduct, and most cases that went to trial ended in acquittals for the defendants, but the prosecutions succeeded in bankrupting AIM. AIM also provoked divisions, even among Lakota sympathetic to their cause. Delphine Red Shirt, then a teenager on the Rosebud Reservation, had contradictory feelings about AIM and the Wounded Knee protest. "On the one hand I identified with those who supported it, and on the other hand I did not like the violence," she remembered in her autobiography, *Bead on an Anthill*. Political stability did not return to Pine Ridge until 1976, when Al Trimble, a respected mixed-blood from the largely traditional community of Wanblee, defeated Wilson in the election for tribal chairman.

The Wounded Knee standoff was, in fact, more important as a symbol to Lakota and to Indians across the nation. Facing down the U.S. government and standing up to protest conditions at Pine Ridge helped restore pride in being Indian and interest in preserving Indian culture. For nearly a century Lakota (and other Indians) had been told that they were "backward," "savage," "primitive," and in need of transformation to become like other Americans. Sun Dances and other Lakota rituals started to become more visible, with more and more Lakota participating. In her autobiography, Mary Crow Dog recalled, "I even saw young boys, ten and eleven years old, having themselves pierced and, after the dance, proudly showing off their scars." Lakota culture began to return to the center of the hoop, of the community, back from the "traditional" communities like Porcupine, Iron Lightning, Cherry Creek, and

Wakpala where it had survived. Pipe ceremonies, prayers, and offerings to Wakan Tanka began to be used at public events and tribal council meetings; even non-Lakota Catholic priests began to invite wicasa wakan to participate in and give blessings at religious ceremonies.

The general resurgence of pride in Indian heritage had other benefits, too. During the late 1960s and early 1970s, the administrations of presidents Lyndon Johnson and Richard Nixon made more money available for programs to improve education, health, and economic development on reservations. On Lakota reservations this led to the founding of tribal colleges like Sinte Gleska University at Rosebud, Oglala Lakota College at Pine Ridge, and Sitting Bull College at Standing Rock. Today, these schools still provide opportunities for Lakota students to earn two- or four-year degrees in a largely Indian setting, as well as courses that teach Lakota language and Lakota culture.

Not all the effects were positive. The increasing visibility and popularity of Indian culture during and after the 1970s also attracted non-Indians. Some merely wanted to learn more about the Lakota and other Native peoples; others, however, were more intrusive. In the past Lakota had had to deal with tourists who wanted to witness "real" Indian rituals, take pictures, and otherwise impose themselves on what were sacred events to the Lakota. Now some non-Indians—hippies, New Agers, and others— wanted to participate. Some even set themselves up as shamans and medicine men, marketing and selling themselves and Indian culture. In June 1993, more than 500 representatives from various Lakota communities met in a conference and issued a "Declaration of War Against Exploiters of Lakota Spirituality," expressing horror at "this disgraceful expropriation of our sacred Lakota traditions."

Lakota were also divided over the increased media attention that they—as the "face" of Native America for many Americans— attracted. The effort to carve a monument to Crazy Horse out of a mountain in the Black Hills (just a few miles from Mount

A likeness of Crazy Horse is being carved into a mountain in the Black Hills. The Lakota have criticized the memorial, which they view as a desecration of their land.

Rushmore) was criticized as a non-Indian attempt to cash in on the Oglala leader's fame and a further desecration of the sacred Black Hills. In 1990, when a major Hollywood studio released the motion picture *Dances with Wolves,* starring Kevin Costner as a disillusioned army officer who befriends the Lakota, Lakotas appreciated the positive portrayal of their people and culture but were amused that the male Indian actors spoke Lakota with a female voice. (Words and grammar in Lakota are gender-specific, meaning that the pronunciation of certain words differs depending on if the speaker is a man or a woman. The language consultant on the movie—a Lakota woman—taught the actors their lines as they would sound if spoken by a woman.)

(*continues on page 104*)

Declaration of War Against Exploiters of Lakota Spirituality (1993)

WHEREAS we represent the recognized traditional spiritual leaders, traditional elders, and grassroots advocates of the Lakota people; and

WHEREAS for too long we have suffered the unspeakable indignity of having our most precious Lakota ceremonies and spiritual practices desecrated, mocked and abused by non-Indian "wannabes," hucksters, cultists, commercial profiteers and self-styled "New Age shamans" and their followers, and . . .

WHEREAS this exponential exploitation of our Lakota spiritual traditions requires that we take immediate action to defend our most precious Lakota spirituality from further contamination, desecration and abuse;

THEREFORE WE RESOLVE AS FOLLOWS:

1. We hereby and henceforth declare war against all persons who persist in exploiting, abusing, and misrepresenting the sacred traditions and spiritual practices of our Lakota, Dakota, and Nakota people.

2. We call upon all our Lakota, Dakota, and Nakota brothers and sisters from reservations, reserves, and traditional communities in the United States and Canada to actively and vocally oppose this alarming take-over and systematic destruction of our sacred traditions.

3. We urge our people to coordinate with their tribal members living in urban areas to identify instances in which our sacred traditions are being abused, and then to resist this abuse, utilizing whatever specific tactics are necessary and sufficient—for example demonstrations, boycotts, press conferences, and acts of direct intervention.

4. We especially urge all our Lakota, Dakota, and Nakota people to take action to prevent our own people from

contributing to and enabling the abuse of our sacred ceremonies and spiritual practices by outsiders; for, as we all know, there are certain ones among our own people who are prostituting our spiritual ways for their own selfish gain, with no regard for the spiritual well-being of the people as a whole.

5. We assert a posture of zero-tolerance for any "white man's shaman" who rises from within our own communities to "authorize" the expropriation of our ceremonial ways by non-Indians; all such "plastic medicine men" are enemies of the Lakota, Dakota, and Nakota people.

6. We urge traditional people, tribal leaders, and governing councils of all other Indian nations to join us in calling for an immediate end to this rampant exploitation of our respective American Indian sacred traditions by issuing statements denouncing such abuse; for it is not the Lakota, Dakota, and Nakota people alone whose spiritual practices are being systematically violated by non-Indians.

7. We urge all our Indian brothers and sisters to act decisively and boldly in our present campaign to end the destruction of our sacred traditions, keeping in mind our highest duty as Indian people: to preserve the purity of our precious traditions for our future generations, so that our children and our children's children will survive and prosper in the sacred manner intended for each of our respective peoples by our Creator.

Wilmer Stampede Mesteth; (Oglala Lakota); Traditional Spiritual Leader & Lakota Culture Instructor; Oglala Lakota College, Pine Ridge, South Dakota

Darrell Standing Elk; (Sicangu Lakota); President, Center for the SPIRIT, San Francisco, California, & Pine Ridge, South Dakota

Phyllis Swift Hawk; (Kul Wicasa Lakota); Tiospaye Wounspe Waokiye; Wanblee, South Dakota

Source: Ward Churchill, *Indians R Us?: Culture and Genocide in Native North America* (Monroe, Maine: Common Courage Press, 1994), pp. 273–77.

(*continued from page 101*)

Nor did increased visibility lift the economic status of many Lakota. Outside of the main towns on the reservations where the tribal headquarters and BIA offices were located—Pine Ridge Village, Fort Yates, Eagle Butte—most Lakota living on their allotments out in the country lacked electricity, running water, and indoor plumbing. Into the 1950s and 1960s, many Lakota still lived in the small log homes their parents and grandparents had built in the early 1900s. Rather than provide electricity and plumbing to thousands of isolated homesteads, the government in the 1960s and early 1970s proposed what was known as "cluster housing"— small housing developments that would group families together and make the task of supplying electricity and water easier and cheaper.

Advocates of cluster housing—including many Lakota tribal councils—argued that the idea would bring people together and improve their overall quality of life. Opponents argued that moving people into cluster housing developments—where there were no businesses and no jobs—and off their land would simply cause problems. Severt Young Bear Sr., a elder from Pine Ridge, told the Wounded Knee Legal Defense Committee that the people in his community "voted 13 times against the cluster housing and in favor of homes being built on an individual's land," but the tribal council ignored their wishes. Cluster housing provided desperately needed homes but over time also led to social problems, including increased drinking, drug use, violence, and even gang activity, while at the same time allowing non-Lakota stockmen to gain access to more Lakota lands as people moved off their allotments. In many ways, even after Wounded Knee it seemed as if little had changed in the relationship between the Lakota, their white neighbors, and the U.S. government.

In reality, however, Lakota defenses of their rights to their culture, land, and self-government had begun long before the 1973 standoff. Within a year of the 1890 Wounded Knee Massacre, Lakota leaders at Pine Ridge and elsewhere had begun to meet to discuss American treaty violations, including, most importantly, the seizure of the Black Hills in 1877. In 1903 Lakota leaders met with U.S. Representative E.W. Martin of South Dakota about the Black Hills, basing their claim on the government's failure to obtain the required three-fourths consent of all Lakota men for the land cession. Unfortunately for the Lakota, that same year the Supreme Court ruled that Congress, as the "guardian" of its Indian "wards," had the power to violate its own treaties, provided that this action was being done in the best interests of the Indians involved. Undeterred, the Lakota in 1922 hired an attorney to legally contest the taking of the Black Hills.

The Black Hills claim wound through the courts for 50 years, repeatedly rejected and just as repeatedly revived. In between, Supreme Court rulings that the government had to pay fair value for any land it obtained from Indians and had to prove it was acting in the Indians' best interest in breaking a treaty or agreement bolstered the Lakota's case. Finally, in 1974 a court ruled that the United States must pay the Lakota $17.5 million plus interest for taking the Black Hills. Following more appeals, the Supreme Court in 1980 ruled that the United States owed the Lakota $106 million. The Lakota, however, refused to take the money. Had the Black Hills claim been settled before 1973, the Lakota most likely would have accepted a financial settlement—the original claim did not seek the return of the Black Hills, just fair compensation. After the Wounded Knee siege, however, no Lakota leader could accept anything less than the return of the land itself. Proposals to return at least part of the Black Hills to the Lakota stalled in Congress. Today, the unclaimed money owed the Lakota continues to accumulate interest in a government account, now amounting to more than $500 million. Lakota tribes also pushed for fair compensation for the lands flooded by Lake Oahe in the late 1950s, eventually gaining a $90.6 million settlement from Congress in 1992.

The Lakota also fought to protect and retain control of lands on their reservations. In 1949 the Pine Ridge tribal council passed

In 1990, hundreds of Lakota reenacted Big Foot's flight from the Seventh Cavalry for the 100th anniversary of the Wounded Knee Massacre.

an ordinance levying a tax on all ranchers who leased Lakota land—many of whom enjoyed Bureau of Indian Affairs leases that gave access to Lakota land at rates far below that charged off the reservation. When stockowners sued to block the tax, a U.S. court ruled that the Pine Ridge council was within its rights under both treaties and the Indian Reorganization Act to levy taxes on reservation land. With many Lakota having fought in or having supported the effort to defend America in World War II—and with many Lakota veterans returning to their communities with increased awareness of the world around them and of their rights as citizens—fewer and fewer Lakota were willing to accept second-class status in America.

It is true, however, that after Wounded Knee the Lakota also began to talk more assertively and confidently—to each other, to the government, and to non-Indians. In 1980, Lakota journalist Tim Giago founded the *Lakota Times,* the first independent, Indian-owned newspaper serving the Lakota, publishing news of interest to Lakota on the reservations and elsewhere; challenging wrongdoing by tribal, state, and federal governments; and condemning racism and prejudice by non-Indians, despite violence that included firebombings, shootings, and death threats. Eventually, the *Lakota Times* (now *Indian Country Today*) became the largest Native American newspaper in the country and spawned the birth of other newspapers on Lakota reservations. Three years after the founding of the *Lakota Times,* Lakota members of the American Indian Movement founded KILI radio, "The Voice of the Lakota Nation," the first Indian-owned and -operated radio station in the United States, broadcasting music and programs in English and Lakota from Porcupine, South Dakota, on the Pine Ridge Reservation with a signal that reaches as far as Cheyenne River, some 200 miles (320 kilometers) away.

Lakota leaders also began to act more assertively to improve economic conditions on the reservations. Besides tribal colleges, Lakota tribal governments in the 1980s and 1990s opened gambling casinos on their reservations (under federal law, Indian tribes are not subject to state laws restricting activities like gambling). Unfortunately, the off-the-beaten track locations of Lakota reservations meant that their casinos were less successful and profitable than other high-profile Indian casinos in California, Connecticut, and Minnesota (and less visible than the casino that Kevin Costner and his brother opened in the more photogenic and tourist-friendly Black Hills town of Deadwood). Lakota leaders also touted their reservations as vacation destinations for history- or nature-minded tourists, and for hunters, fishermen, and other outdoor recreation enthusiasts, and supported efforts to attract manufacturers and other businesses.

Finally, in 1986 Lakota from several reservations organized the Big Foot Memorial Ride, a three-week, 250-mile (400-kilometer) pilgrimage on horseback from the site of Sitting Bull's death to the site of the Wounded Knee Massacre. The intent, according to ride organizers, was to bring healing to the spirits of those who died at Wounded Knee, as well as to the survivors and their descendants, and to help transmit Lakota values and culture to future generations. The fifth Big Foot Memorial Ride, held in 1990 on the 100th anniversary of the massacre, attracted nearly 300 riders from all the Lakota reservations, braving temperatures as low as 30 degrees below zero (–34° C) to perform what most saw as a sacred task. That same year, pressure from Lakota media and grassroots organizations finally led to a congressional apology for the Wounded Knee Massacre.

The Lakota Today

Today, the ghosts of the past still haunt Pine Ridge, Cheyenne River, Standing Rock, and the other Lakota reservations. Some of these ghosts are visible, like the Sitting Bull memorial at the site where the Hunkpapa leader is claimed to be buried near Mobridge, South Dakota, or the mass grave and memorial to members of Big Foot's band who were killed at Wounded Knee. Others are unseen but constantly present, as in the flooded Lakota land resting beneath the waters of Lake Oahe. Still others live on in the memories and stories of the Lakota themselves—tales of events in the timeless past of White Buffalo Woman; the distant past of buffalo-hunting days, of Red Cloud, Crazy Horse, and the Little Big Horn; or the more recent past amid the struggles of reservation life: allotment, boarding schools, the Indian Reorganization Act, and the political disputes that led to the Wounded Knee standoff.

The mass burial site of 146 of the American Indians killed in the Wounded Knee Massacre is shown above.

The legacies these ghosts left behind shape Lakota society, for better or worse. Once, the Lakota were among the most powerful and prosperous peoples in America; today, several Lakota reservations rank among the most impoverished communities in the United States. According to the United States Census Bureau, in 2008 Ziebach County, South Dakota (part of the Cheyenne River Reservation), ranked as the poorest county in the country, with 54.4 percent of its households having incomes below the poverty line; Shannon County, South Dakota (part of the Pine Ridge Reservation) ranked fourth.

Every day, Lakota struggle with the dilemma of how to reconcile Lakota values and beliefs with a modern world and modern economy. As Guy Dull Knife Jr. put it in *The Dull Knifes of Pine Ridge,* "If we are to make it as a people, our children must know about computers and the Eagle Dance. . . . They need to know how to read and write and balance a checkbook, but they must also know who they are and where they are from."

The cost of living on reservations is high; most large retail outlets are dozens to more than a hundred miles distant in cities like Bismarck and Rapid City, yet employment and income on the reservations are far lower than in those cities. Though this problem is shared to some extent by nearly all rural residents in North and South Dakota, for the Lakota, it is magnified by the continuing emphasis on being a "good relative" and being generous to those in need. Lakota business owners often struggle to balance the need to make a profit with the desire not to be seen as greedy. "It's harder with us if you have some traditional values," a woman who manufactured picture frames but ended up giving most of them away explained in Kathleen Ann Pickering's book, *Lakota Culture, World Economy.* "I think it's why the concept of business hasn't gone over so well among Indians, is the value system is different." In *Standing in the Light: A Lakota Way of Seeing,* Severt Young Bear adds that "the traditional way of thinking tells us that when you have material possessions, the best thing you can do with them is to give them away, especially to those who are without or are having a hard time. . . . A leader is not the guy who can store up and keep lots of things, but instead someone who will share them with the people." Lakota businesses also often face discrimination and reluctance to lend money from non-Indian banks and other financial institutions.

Finding steady employment is also a problem. Many Lakota work for either the tribal or federal government or for the schools or missions operated by religious denominations. Much of the other wage work available tends to be manual, seasonal labor, either in agriculture, construction, or tourism. Although all the Lakota tribes operate casinos, their out-of-the-way location limits the jobs and income they provide, while many Lakota worry about the social problems that could come from gambling. Other Lakota, especially women, are self-employed in manufacturing arts and

Who Is Lakota?

Historically, the Lakota were united by kinship (which could take the form of actual "blood" or biological ties, or the adoption of outsiders who were not Lakota by birth or ancestry) and culture. One could not "become" a Lakota the way an immigrant can become a citizen of the United States today. In the pre-reservation era, the Lakota, unlike modern nations, did not have a centralized government with the power to decide who was and was not Lakota. Instead of being built from the top down, Lakota society was constructed from the bottom up. One became Lakota by being accepted as a member of a Lakota family and by fulfilling the proper social obligations toward other members of one's family and other relatives and individuals within the larger Lakota community. As a result, people who were not born Lakota could become Lakota—even individuals captured from communities with which the Lakota were at war.

When the Lakota fell under increasing U.S. government control in the late 1800s, this structure began to change. As the Lakota became more dependent on government rations and as the government began to split up reservations formerly owned in common by all Lakota into individual plots of private property, U.S. officials increasingly began to regulate and restrict the number of people considered Lakota or who sought to become part of Lakota society—as did emerging

crafts items, such as beadwork, clothes, or star quilts (patchwork quilts that became popular—and necessary—among the Lakota once buffalo hides were no longer available; the name comes from the geometric patterns on them), using skills handed down from generation to generation. Even so, unemployment on many reservations exceeds 50 percent (and in some cases may reach as high tribal councils and other forms of tribal government among the Lakota.

Today, the tribal government on each Lakota reservation determines the qualifications a person must meet to be considered a tribal member. At the Cheyenne River Reservation—home to the Miniconjou, Oohenonpa (or Two Kettle), Itazipco (Sans Arcs or Without Bows), and Sihasapa (or Blackfoot) Lakota—individuals must have at least one parent who is an enrolled member of the tribe. Children born to parents who reside on the reservation must be approved by a majority vote of the tribal council; children born to parents living off the reservation must be approved by a two-thirds vote. At Standing Rock—home to Hunkpapa and Sihasapa Lakota—applicants for enrollment must be able to demonstrate that they are at least one-fourth Lakota by descent and have at least one grandparent or parent who is a member of the Standing Rock Sioux Tribe.

Tribal membership provides certain rights, including voting rights in tribal elections, access to tribally provided services, and other benefits tied to tribal affiliation. But it also raises troubling questions for many Lakota (and other Indians) over the seemingly arbitrary nature of legal definitions of identity, the lack of cultural markers such as fluency in a native language, and the possibility that one's status as a Lakota could be jeopardized by the need to move from the reservation for educational or career opportunities.

as 80 to 90 percent), forcing many Lakota to confront the choice of leaving their community to find work off the reservation or staying and facing uncertain economic prospects.

Low income levels and the limited nutritional choices available in largely rural or small town communities have also led to health problems. With few options beyond fast-food outlets or small grocery or convenience stores, diabetes has become a significant concern, with several Lakota tribes reporting diabetes among nearly half the adult population. Alcoholism and other forms of substance abuse also continue to be serious issues in many reservation communities. To combat these problems, a movement has emerged among some Lakota to move out of cluster housing and back to the land in an effort to return to a healthier lifestyle. In recent years many Lakota tribes have also sought to consolidate and build the tribal land base by reacquiring reservation land lost to non-Indians and keeping existing Indian-owned land within the tribe.

The back-to-the-land movement also marks another distinctive feature of modern Lakota life—the persistence of traditional Lakota social and cultural values. Children are still prized and enjoy a far larger array of close relatives than most non-Indian children. Many Lakota boys and girls spend part of their childhood living with grandparents or aunts and uncles as well as with their parents. Each summer Lakota reservations host multiple powwows—usually one in each reservation district (or community) as well a larger tribal powwow that often attracts visitors and Indian participants from across the Northern Plains and beyond. Smaller, family or community-level events—both social and spiritual—take place throughout the year, with the most important and sacred events, such as the annual Sun Dance, regarded as off-limits to tourists and non-Lakota.

Although most Lakota today remain at least nominal members of some mainstream Christian denomination, increasing numbers blend these faiths with older Lakota spiritual traditions, or with the tenets of other Native American religions such as the Native American Church, a national Indian religious denomination that combines elements of Christianity with the use of peyote (a hallucinogenic cactus) as a sacrament similar to the Catholic Eucharist. Peyotism and Lakota spirituality have even been incorporated in programs targeting substance abuse and other social problems in reservation communities.

Lakota Indians dance at a powwow on the Pine Ridge Reservation. As more Lakota become "mainstream," the challenge is to preserve the cultural traditions and language of the tribe.

Perhaps the greatest cultural challenge facing the Lakota is the preservation and perpetuation of the Lakota language. Even with the renewed appreciation and support for Lakota culture among families, in schools, in public events, and in terms of tribal support, Lakota language proficiency has been steadily dwindling, particularly as older tribal members born and raised before the arrival of television on the reservations die and are replaced by younger generations familiar with radio, television, and the Internet. According to the 2000 U.S. census, just 14 percent of the Indian population on the five Lakota reservations identified themselves as Lakota speakers, ranging from a high of 25 percent at Pine Ridge to a low of just 4 percent at Lower Brulé. Despite Lakota language programs in elementary and secondary schools, an increasing number of Lakota children grow up in homes where English is the primary language and true fluency in Lakota is increasingly rare. For children growing up off the reservation in largely non-Indian communities where Lakota is not taught in public or private schools, the difficulty of developing language proficiency is even greater.

Despite these issues, it seems clear that the Lakota as a people are not going to disappear. In fact, the Lakota community as a whole is growing larger and faster than it has since the early 1800s. After recovering from a population nadir in the early 1900s (when some government officials predicted the eventual extinction of all Indians), the Lakota today are among the fastest-growing ethnic groups in the United States, with a population of more than 75,000, according to the 2000 census. The Oglala Sioux Tribe alone had an enrollment of more than 47,000 in October 2008. Overall, the Lakota population in South Dakota is expected to double between 2000 and 2030.

The challenge for Lakota tribes today remains the same as it has been for much of the past century: to provide opportunities and a standard of living for their members that allows them to thrive in both the Indian and white worlds. One path to doing so, many Lakota believe, is to return to their philosophical and social origins as a "buffalo nation." Each year, Lakota youth participate in a relay race around the Black Hills that commemorates the race between the four-legged and the two-legged that earned the Lakota the right to eat the buffalo. Many children still receive traditional Lakota names—used on special or ceremonial occasions—to go along with their "official" given and family names.

Finally, in 1994 a white buffalo calf was born on a ranch operated by a non-Indian family near Janesville, Wisconsin. Named "Miracle," word of the birth spread quickly throughout Indian country, with Lakota and other Indians traveling to southern

Wisconsin to view the calf. For the Lakota, "Miracle" summoned up memories of White Buffalo Woman and her gift to the Lakota people. Today, all seven Lakota tribes are members of the Inter-tribal Bison Cooperative, an alliance of 57 tribes seeking to restore buffalo to their natural habitats on reservation land, and all five contemporary Lakota tribes maintain tribal bison herds that are used as a source of food, a tourist attraction, and a means of transmitting Lakota culture to future generations. In this way, the Lakota are seeking to mend the sacred hoop and restore harmony among the Lakota people themselves, between the natural (and supernatural) world the Lakota live in, and between all peoples everywhere.

Chronology

1600s   The Lakota reside mainly in the prairie region of south-western Minnesota and eastern South Dakota.

Late 1600s   French explorers hear of a people called the "Nadouessioux" (Little Snakes) living to the west of the Ojibway of Wisconsin and Minnesota.

Early 1700s   The Lakota acquire their first horses and begin to edge farther west into the buffalo country of the Great Plains.

Timeline

1866

Treaty negotiations between the United States and the Lakota break down after troops are sent to occupy the Bozeman Trail, beginning the conflict known as Red Cloud's War

1868

The Fort Laramie Treaty of 1868 establishes the Great Sioux Reservation

1775–1776

A party of Lakota under Standing Bull reaches the Black Hills

1775

1870

1600s

The Lakota reside mainly in the prairie region of south-western Minnesota and eastern South Dakota

1851

The Fort Laramie Treaty of 1851 (or Horse Creek Treaty) sets boundaries for Plains Indian tribes and promises compensation for damages caused by emigrants

1877

The United States seizes the Black Hills from the Lakota. Crazy Horse surrenders and is later killed by a U.S. soldier while being arrested

1757	The first mention of a mounted Lakota war party on a Lakota winter count (a pictorial depiction of each year's most significant event recorded on a buffalo hide).
1775–1776	A party of Lakota under Standing Bull reaches the Black Hills.
1804	The Lewis and Clark Expedition meets with a Brulé Lakota band along the Missouri River in what is now South Dakota.
1825	The United States and the Lakota sign a treaty of peace and friendship.
1840s	Increasing emigrant traffic on the Oregon Trail begins to generate tensions between the Lakota and Americans.
1851	The Fort Laramie Treaty of 1851 (or Horse Creek Treaty) sets boundaries for Plains Indian tribes and promises

December 29, 1890

The U.S. Army massacres a band of Ghost Dancers led by the Miniconjou Lakota Big Foot at Wounded Knee

1934

Congress passes the Indian Reorganization Act (Wheeler-Howard Act) with the goal of giving greater powers of self-rule to Indian tribes

1980

U.S. Supreme Court affirms the 1974 Black Hills ruling and awards the Lakota $106 million

1900   **1990**

1889

The Sioux Bill of 1889 breaks up the Great Sioux Reservation into five separate reservations

1973

Oglala Lakota and AIM occupy Wounded Knee for 71 days, protesting U.S. treaty violations and the Pine Ridge tribal administration of Richard Wilson

1990

Congress issues a formal apology for the 1890 Wounded Knee Massacre compensation for damages caused by emigrants; it also marks the beginnings of U.S. efforts to "civilize" Plains Indians.

1854 After a Lakota shoots an emigrant's stray cow, fighting breaks out between Lakotas and soldiers near Fort Laramie; a 29-man detachment of soldiers under Lt. John Grattan is wiped out.

1855 Army troops attack a Lakota camp at Ash Hollow, Nebraska, killing nearly 100 men, women, and children.

Early 1860s Anglo-Indian conflicts in Minnesota and Colorado and along the Platte River create hostilities between the Lakota and the United States.

1863 The Bozeman Trail, an emigrant road to Montana, is blazed through the Powder River Country—part of the Lakota homeland and the richest hunting region on the Northern Plains.

1866 Treaty negotiations between the United States and the Lakota break down after troops are sent to occupy the Bozeman Trail, beginning the conflict known as Red Cloud's War.

1868 After several military defeats the United States agrees to abandon the Bozeman Trail; the Fort Laramie Treaty of 1868 establishes the Great Sioux Reservation.

1869 The first transcontinental railroad is completed.

1874 A military expedition under Lt. Col. George A. Custer discovers gold in the Black Hills.

1875 As negotiations over the sale of the Black Hills break down, the United States orders all Lakota to report to their agencies by January 31, 1876, or be considered hostile.

1876 Army troops attack Lakota and Cheyenne villages, including an attack on a village on the Little Big Horn River on June 25 and 26 in which 263 soldiers of the Seventh Cavalry are killed.

1877 The United States seizes the Black Hills from the Lakota.

Crazy Horse surrenders and is later killed by a U.S. soldier while being arrested.

1881   The last Lakota holdouts under Sitting Bull surrender at Fort Buford, Dakota Territory.

1887   The General Allotment Act (or Dawes Act) proposes the breakup of Indian reservations into separate, privately owned parcels of land issued to Indian families.

1889   The Sioux Bill of 1889 breaks up the Great Sioux Reservation into five separate reservations; rations due the Lakota are cut immediately afterward.

Lakota delegations travel west to Nevada to investigate a new Indian religion (the Ghost Dance).

1890   Many Lakota participate in Ghost Dances; army troops are dispatched to Lakota reservations.

1890   December 15   Standing Rock Indian police sent to arrest Sitting Bull kill the Hunkpapa leader.
December 19   The U.S. Army massacres a band of Ghost Dancers led by the Miniconjou Lakota Big Foot at Wounded Knee.

1917–1918   Lakota serve in the U.S. military during World War I.

1922   Attorneys for the Lakota file suit in U.S. court over land seizures and other treaty violations by the U.S. government.

1934   Congress passes the Indian Reorganization Act (Wheeler-Howard Act) with the goal of giving greater powers of self-rule to Indian tribes.

Lakota reservations hold elections on whether to accept the IRA; referendums pass on all Lakota reservations despite low voter turnout.

**1950s–
1960s**   Federal relocation programs provide assistance to many Lakota to move off reservations to cities across the United States.

1964 Oglala Lakota Billy Mills wins the gold medal in the 10,000-meter run at the Tokyo Olympics.

1968 American Indian Movement (AIM) is founded in Minneapolis, Minnesota.

1970 Sinte Gleska (Spotted Tail) University is founded on Rosebud Reservation.

1972 Raymond Yellow Thunder (Oglala Lakota) dies in Gordon, Nebraska; AIM joins Oglala Lakota in protesting racism in Gordon.

Lakota participate in the Trail of Broken Treaties protest, culminating in the occupation of the Bureau of Indian Affairs headquarters in Washington, D.C.

1973 Oglala Lakota and AIM occupy Wounded Knee for 71 days, protesting U.S. treaty violations and the Pine Ridge tribal administration of Richard Wilson.

1974 The Indian Claims Commission makes a preliminary decision to award the Lakota $17.5 million plus interest for the illegal 1877 taking of the Black Hills.

1980 U.S. Supreme Court affirms the 1974 Black Hills ruling and awards the Lakota $106 million.

Lakota Times, the first independent Lakota-owned newspaper, begins publication.

1983 KILI radio (90.1 FM) begins broadcasting.

1986 First Big Foot Memorial Ride is held.

1990 Congress issues a formal apology for the 1890 Wounded Knee Massacre.

Glossary

akicita   A Lakota word for a member of a warrior society charged with keeping order in a camp or during hunts or camp movements.

American Indian Movement (AIM)   Native American protest group founded in 1968 in Minneapolis. In the early 1970s members of AIM (including some Lakota) led protests over conditions on Lakota reservations and in South Dakota, including the 1973 occupation of Wounded Knee.

blotahunka   Lakota term for a war leader during the nineteenth century.

Bureau of Indian Affairs   The U.S. government agency charged with handling matters related to Indians in the United States.

Ghost Dance   An apocalyptic Native American religion in the late nineteenth century, originating with the Paiute of Nevada. It predicted the disappearance of whites and the return of the pre-white Indian world. The Lakota adoption of the Ghost Dance in 1890 was one of the events that led to the Wounded Knee Massacre.

hanbleceyapi   A Lakota term that translates roughly as "crying for a vision"; also known as a vision quest.

Indian Reorganization Act (IRA)   A law (also known as the Wheeler-Howard Act) passed by Congress in 1934. Intended to restore powers of self-government to Indian tribes, the IRA caused much controversy and disunity within Lakota tribes.

itancan   The leader of a Lakota *tiyospaye,* or band.

pejuta winyela   A Lakota term for a medicine woman; a woman with *wakan* powers skilled in using herbs for healing.

shirtwearer   During the mid- to late nineteenth century, one of a select group of young men (usually four in each Lakota tribe) charged with being a peacemaker and caring for the well-being of their community.

Sun Dance   The most important collective tribal spiritual ritual of the Lakota, usually held once a year in late summer. Prohibited by the U.S.

government for nearly 50 years, the Sun Dance has recently enjoyed a renaissance in many Lakota communities.

tiyospaye   A Lakota term for a collection of families (or band) that camped and hunted together.

wakan   Lakota word for "holy."

Wakan Tanka   Lakota term for "great mystery," or the totality of all *wakan* powers in the universe.

wakiconza   Lakota word for the individual in charge of managing the day-to-day affairs of a *tiyospaye;* a sort of camp administrator.

wasicus   Lakota word for white men.

wicasa wakan   Lakota word for a holy man or shaman; a person with special *wakan* power.

Bibliography

Albers, Patricia, and Beatrice Medicine. *The Hidden Half: Studies of Plains Indian Women*. Lanham, Md.: University Press of America, 1983.

Bettelyoun, Susan Bordeaux, and Josephine Waggoner. *With My Own Eyes: A Lakota Woman Tells Her People's History*. Edited by Emily Levine. Lincoln, Neb.: University of Nebraska Press, 1998.

Biolsi, Thomas. *Organizing the Lakota: The Political Economy of the New Deal on the Pine Ridge and Rosebud Reservations*. Tucson: The University of Arizona Press, 1992.

Bray, Kingsley. *Crazy Horse: A Lakota Life*. Norman, Okla.: University of Oklahoma Press, 2006.

Burnette, Robert, and John Koster. *The Road to Wounded Knee*. New York: Bantam Books, 1974.

Churchill, Ward. *Indians R Us?: Culture and Genocide in Native North America*. Monroe, Maine: Common Courage Press, 1994.

Crow Dog, Mary, with Richard Erdoes. *Lakota Woman*. New York: Grove Weidenfeld, 1990.

DeMallie, Raymond J., and Douglas R. Parks, eds. *Sioux Indian Religion: Tradition and Innovation*. Norman, Okla.: University of Oklahoma Press, 1987.

DeMallie, Raymond J. "The Sioux at the Time of European Contact: An Ethnohistorical Problem." In *New Perspectives on Native North America: Cultures, Histories, and Representations*. Edited by Sergei A. Kan and Pauline Turner Strong. Lincoln: University of Nebraska Press, 2006, 239–260.

Dewing, Rolland. *Wounded Knee: The Meaning and Significance of the Second Incident*. New York: Irvington Publishers, 1985.

Franco, Jere' Bishop. *Crossing the Pond: The Native American Effort in World War II*. Denton, Tex.: University of North Texas Press, 1999.

Frazier, Ian. *On the Rez*. New York: Farrar, Straus and Giroux, 2000.

Giago, Tim. *Notes from Indian Country, Volume 1*. Pierre, S.D.: State Publishing Company, 1984.

Gibbon, Guy. *The Sioux: The Dakota and Lakota Nations*. Malden, Mass.: Blackwell Publishing, 2003.

Gray, John S. *Centennial Campaign: The Sioux War of 1876*. Fort Collins, Colo.: Old Army Press, 1976.

Greene, Candace S., and Russell Thornton, eds. *The Year the Stars Fell: Lakota Winter Counts at the Smithsonian*. Lincoln: University of Nebraska Press, 2007.

Greene, Jerome. *Lakota and Cheyenne: Indian Views of the Great Sioux War, 1876–1877*. Norman, Okla.: University of Oklahoma Press, 1994.

Hyde, George. *Red Cloud's Folk: A History of the Oglala Sioux Indians*. Norman, Okla.: University of Oklahoma Press, 1937.

_____. *A Sioux Chronicle*. Norman, Okla.: University of Oklahoma Press, 1956.

_____. *Spotted Tail's Folk: A History of the Brulé Sioux*. Norman, Okla.: University of Oklahoma Press, 1961.

Iverson, Peter. *When Indians Became Cowboys: Native Peoples and Cattle Ranching in the American West*. Norman, Okla.: University of Oklahoma Press, 1994.

_____. *"We Are Still Here": American Indians in the Twentieth Century*. Wheeling, Ill.: Harlan Davidson, 1998.

Krouse, Susan Applegate. *North American Indians in the Great War*. Lincoln: University of Nebraska Press, 2007.

Lawson, Michael L. *Dammed Indians: The Pick-Sloan Plan and the Missouri River Sioux, 1944–1980*. Norman, Okla.: University of Oklahoma Press, 1982.

Lazarus, Edward. *Black Hills, White Justice: The Sioux Nation versus the United States, 1775 to the Present*. Lincoln: University of Nebraska Press, 1991.

Mails, Thomas E. *Fools Crow*. Lincoln: University of Nebraska Press, 1979.

McDonnell, Janet A. *The Dispossession of the American Indian, 1887–1934*. Bloomington, Ind.: Indiana University Press, 1991.

Means, Russell, with Marvin J. Wolf. *Where White Men Fear to Tread: The Autobiography of Russell Means*. New York: St. Martin's Press, 1995.

Medicine, Beatrice. "Lakota Star Quilts: Commodity, Ceremony, and Economic Development." In *To Honor and Comfort: Native Quilting Traditions*. Edited by Marsha L. McDowell and C. Kurt Dewhurst. Santa Fe: Museum of New Mexico Press and Michigan State University Museum, 1997, 111–117.

_____. *Drinking and Sobriety among the Lakota Sioux*. Lanham, Md.: AltaMira Press, 2007.

Mooney, James. *The Ghost Dance Religion and Wounded Knee.* Mineola, N.Y.: Dover Publications, 1973.

Neihardt, John G. *The Sixth Grandfather: Black Elk's Teachings Given to John G. Neihardt.* Edited by Raymond J. DeMallie. Lincoln: University of Nebraska Press, 1984.

Ostler, Jeffrey. *The Plains Sioux and U.S. Colonialism from Lewis and Clark to Wounded Knee.* New York: Cambridge University Press, 2004.

Penman, Sarah, ed. *Honor the Grandmothers: Dakota and Lakota Women Tell Their Stories.* St. Paul, Minn.: Minnesota Historical Society Press, 2000.

Petrillo, Larissa. *Being Lakota: Identity and Tradition on Pine Ridge Reservation.* Lincoln: University of Nebraska Press, 2007.

Pickering, Kathleen Ann. *Lakota Culture, World Economy.* Lincoln: University of Nebraska Press, 2000.

Powers, Marla N. *Oglala Women: Myth, Ritual, and Reality.* Chicago: The University of Chicago Press, 1986.

Price, Catherine. *The Oglala People, 1841–1879: A Political History.* Lincoln: University of Nebraska Press, 1996.

Red Shirt, Delphine. *Bead on an Anthill: A Lakota Childhood.* Lincoln: University of Nebraska Press, 1998.

Reinhardt, Akim D. *Ruling Pine Ridge: Oglala Lakota Politics from the IRA to Wounded Knee.* Lubbock: Texas Tech University Press, 2007.

Robertson, Paul. *The Power of the Land: Identity, Ethnicity, and Class among the Oglala Lakota.* New York: Routledge, 2002.

St. Pierre, Mark. *Madonna Swan: A Lakota Woman's Story.* Norman, Okla.: University of Oklahoma Press, 1991.

Standing Bear, Luther. *My People the Sioux.* New York: Houghton Mifflin, 1928; reprint, Lincoln: University of Nebraska Press, 1975.

———. *Land of the Spotted Eagle.* New York: Houghton Mifflin, 1933; reprint, Lincoln: University of Nebraska Press, 1978.

Starita, Joe. *The Dull Knifes of Pine Ridge: A Lakota Odyssey.* New York: Putnam, 1995.

Utley, Robert M. *The Lance and the Shield: The Life and Times of Sitting Bull.* New York: Ballantine Books, 1993.

Valandra, Edward Charles. *Not Without Our Consent: Lakota Resistance to Termination, 1950–59.* Urbana, Ill.: University of Illinois Press, 2006.

Wagoner, Paula L. *"They Treated Us Just Like Indians": The Worlds of Bennett County, South Dakota.* Lincoln: University of Nebraska Press, 2002.

Walker, James R. *Lakota Belief and Ritual.* Edited by Raymond J. DeMallie and Elaine A. Jahner. Lincoln: University of Nebraska Press, 1980.

_____. *Lakota Society*. Edited by Raymond J. DeMallie. Lincoln: University of Nebraska Press, 1982.

Warrior, Robert, and Paul Chaat Smith. *Like a Hurricane: The Indian Movement from Alcatraz to Wounded Knee*. New York: The New Press, 1996.

Wood, W. Raymond. "Plains Trade in Prehistoric and Protohistoric Intertribal Relations." In *Anthropology on the Great Plains*. Edited by W. Raymond Wood and Margot Liberty. Lincoln: University of Nebraska Press, 1980, 98–109.

Young Bear, Severt, and R.D. Theisz. *Standing in the Light: A Lakota Way of Seeing*. Lincoln: University of Nebraska Press, 1994.

Further Resources

Books

Bettelyoun, Susan Bordeaux, and Josephine Waggoner. *With My Own Eyes: A Lakota Woman Tells Her People's History.* Edited by Emily Levine. Lincoln: University of Nebraska Press, 1998.

Bray, Kingsley. *Crazy Horse: A Lakota Life.* Norman, Okla.: University of Oklahoma Press, 2006. A recent, thorough biography of the Oglala Lakota leader.

Crow Dog, Mary, with Richard Erdoes. *Lakota Woman.* New York: Grove Weidenfeld, 1990.

Gibbon, Guy. *The Sioux: The Dakota and Lakota Nations.* Malden, Mass.: Blackwell Publishing, 2003.

Neihardt, John G. *The Sixth Grandfather: Black Elk's Teachings Given to John G. Neihardt.* Edited by Raymond J. DeMallie. Lincoln: University of Nebraska Press, 1984.

Standing Bear, Luther. *My People the Sioux.* New York: Houghton Mifflin, 1928; reprint, Lincoln: University of Nebraska Press, 1975.

Utley, Robert M. *The Lance and the Shield: The Life and Times of Sitting Bull.* New York: Ballantine Books, 1993.

Warrior, Robert, and Paul Chaat Smith. *Like a Hurricane: The Indian Movement from Alcatraz to Wounded Knee.* New York: The New Press, 1996.

DVDs

Homeland. Produced, directed, and edited by Jilann Spitzmiller and Hank Rogerson in association with the Independent Television Service, 60 minutes, 1999. Traces the experiences of four Lakota families from the Pine Ridge Indian Reservation and their effort to hold on to their culture.

Wiping the Tears of Seven Generations. Kifaru Productions in association with Eagle Heart Productions; directed by Gary Rhine and Fidel Moreno, 57 minutes, 1992. Tells the story of the first Big Foot Memorial Rides to commemorate the 1890 massacre at Wounded Knee.

Web Sites

Tribal Web Sites

Cheyenne River Sioux
http://www.sioux.org
Web site of the Cheyenne River Sioux Tribe. Contains links on Cheyenne River Sioux history and culture, tribal government, and reservation news.

Lower Brule Sioux
http://www.lbst.org
Web site of the Lower Brulé Sioux Tribe.

Oglala Sioux
http://www.oglalalakotanation.org
Web site of the Oglala Sioux Tribe of the Pine Ridge Indian Reservation.

Rosebud Sioux
http://www.rosebudsiouxtribe-nsn.gov
Web site of the Rosebud Sioux Tribe.

Standing Rock Sioux
http://www.standingrock.org
Web site of the Standing Rock Sioux Tribe

Other Web Sites

Akta Lakota Museum and Cultural Center
http://www.aktalakota.org
Web site of the Akta Lakota Museum and Cultural Center, operated by St. Joseph's Indian School in Chamberlain, South Dakota.

Dakota-Sioux Language
http://www.native-languages.org/dakota
Web site contains links to and information on Lakota and Dakota language resources, including word lists and pronunciation aids.

Father Bucko's Mighty Home Page
http://puffin.creighton.edu/bucko
Homepage of Father Raymond Bucko, a faculty member at Creighton University in Omaha, Nebraska. Site includes an extensive bibliography on Lakota history and culture.

Lakota Country Times
http://www.lakotacountrytimes.com
Lakota-owned and -operated newspaper covering news and events of interest to residents of Lakota reservations.

Picture Credits

Index

About the Contributors

XXXXXXXXXXXXXXX

FRANK RZECZKOWSKI is a visiting assistant professor of history at Xavier University in Cincinnati, Ohio. His research focuses on Northern Plains Indians during the nineteenth and twentieth centuries. His book *"For the Protection of Our People": Tribes, Indians, and Community on the Northern Plains, 1800–1925* is scheduled to be published by the University Press of Kansas.

Series editor **PAUL C. ROSIER** received his Ph.D. in American History from the University of Rochester in 1998. Dr. Rosier currently serves as associate professor of history at Villanova University (Villanova, Pennsylvania), where he teaches Native American History, American Environmental History, Global Environmental Justice Movements, History of American Capitalism, and World History.

In 2001, the University of Nebraska Press published his first book, *Rebirth of the Blackfeet Nation, 1912–1954*; in 2003, Greenwood Press published *Native American Issues* as part of its Contemporary Ethnic American Issues series. In 2006, he coedited an international volume called *Echoes from the Poisoned Well: Global Memories of Environmental Injustice*. Dr. Rosier has also published articles in the *American Indian Culture and Research Journal*, the *Journal of American Ethnic History*, and *The Journal of American History*. His *Journal of American History* article, entitled "They Are Ancestral Homelands: Race, Place, and Politics in Cold War Native America, 1945–1961," was selected for inclusion in *The Ten Best History Essays of 2006–2007*, published by Palgrave MacMillan in 2008 and it won the Western History Association's 2007 Arrell Gibson Award for Best Essay on the history of Native Americans. His latest book, *Serving Their Country: American Indian Politics and Patriotism in the Twentieth Century* (Harvard University Press) is winner of the 2010 Labriola Center American Indian National Book Award.